CHAIRMAKING
& DESIGN

CHAIRMAKING
& DESIGN

Jeff Miller

The Taunton Press

COVER PHOTOGRAPHER: Tanya Tucka

Taunton
BOOKS & VIDEOS
for fellow enthusiasts

First printing: July 1997
Printed in the United States of America

A FINE WOODWORKING Book
FINE WOODWORKING® is a trademark of The Taunton Press, Inc.,
registered in the U.S. Patent and Trademark Office.

The Taunton Press, Inc., 63 South Main Street,
PO Box 5506, Newtown, CT 06470-5506

Library of Congress Cataloging-in-Publication Data

Miller, Jeff, 1956-
    Chairmaking & design / Jeff Miller.
        p.   cm.
    "A Fine Woodworking book"—T.p. verso.
    Includes index.
    ISBN 1-56158-158-5
    1. Chairs. 2. Furniture making. I. Title.
TT197.5.C45M55   1997   97-16538
    684.1'3—dc21   CIP

To Becky, Isaac, and Ariel

CONTENTS

ACKNOWLEDGMENTS

I am grateful to the woodworkers and museum curators who shared photographs of their chairs and those in their care.

Thanks to all of those people who shared their time and expertise so generously and to those who listened patiently to my ideas and encouraged or discouraged as needed—I'm especially grateful for the new friendships that resulted from this endeavor.

Thanks to Rick Peters, Joanne Renna, and others at The Taunton Press for their unwavering support, humor, and patience throughout the process and for having faith that my obsession might be converted into a worthwhile book.

Thanks to Tanya, whose ability to turn even mundane shop operations into terrific photos amazes me.

And love and gratitude to my parents, who have never lost faith in what I do—no matter how strange.

A Word about Safety

Woodworking is inherently dangerous. Shop safety involves many issues. Knowledge and experience are parts of safe work, but these do not prevent accidents. Attitude and approach are also very important. Constant awareness of the dangers (to limb and life) is essential.

Please familiarize yourself with safe procedures for both hand and power tools. Never override these safety measures out of laziness, fatigue, anger, impatience, or desire for speed. It is easy to bypass the safe way to work, and this is often the precursor to an accident.

If you are not comfortable with a procedure that you see in this book (or elsewhere), find another way to do it. If it seems dangerous to you, it probably is.

INTRODUCTION

Most woodworkers are both fascinated with and in awe of chairmaking. Chairs are seen as the pinnacle of the woodworker's art and impossibly complex to make. Why is this? Chairs can be simple, complicated, or anything in between, just like any other piece of furniture. Even so, few choose to enter the realm of compound angles, curves, and comfort.

Part of the reason is that chairs are different from other kinds of furniture. Chairs challenge us with angles and/or curves to deal with and all of those joints. And chairs usually come in sets, which makes for an even bigger project. But there are also more elusive challenges. We want chairs to be many things. We want them to be comfortable, which is a challenge because of the variety of ways we sit in chairs and the variety of people who may sit in them. We want chairs to be durable, which is also a challenge because of how we use and abuse them. And we want chairs to look good. In fact, how we want chairs to look is perhaps the biggest challenge of all. More than any other type of furniture, chairs are a reflection of the taste, status, and wealth of the owner. Chairs have always been designed to reflect and enhance these elements.

My fascination with chairs began innocently enough. I needed a couple of chairs for my kitchen table. A book of simple plans, a few weekends of work, and I had them—a pair of really uncomfortable chairs. (They didn't last long either.) This was long before I was making furniture professionally, and my next venture into the fray came in my second year in business. A customer commissioned a dining table and wanted to know if I could do the chairs as well. Of course I could. But having been humbled once, I started to look into what was involved a little more closely. And the more I saw, the more intrigued I became.

Chair design at its most basic is an attempt to solve very practical problems: how to make a seat that is both comfortable and durable. An incredible variety of chair forms attempt to solve these problems. But chair design moves very quickly beyond this into the very unusual territory of appearance. Here we find elements of power, philosophy, and history and also some whimsy and wonderful innovation, all mixed together in designing the way the chair looks. This challenge is what makes chair design such a special thing.

I ultimately designed a chair not unlike the slat-back chair (see Chapter 6) for my customer. I've gone on to design dozens more chairs. And my fascination (obsession?) with chair design, history, and culture has grown steadily.

I think of this book as something like a book of musical études (my former career was as a professional musician). The chairs are complete works by themselves but are also designed to increase mastery of a variety of skills. They increase in complexity as the book progresses. There is also an assumption that some of the skills discussed in earlier chapters will be familiar by the later chapters. I doubt many people will make all of the chairs in the book, but it would be a rather complete course in chairmaking to do so because most of the basic structural types are covered.

1
BASICS OF CHAIR DESIGN

Chair design poses three fundamental challenges: making the chair comfortable, durable, and good-looking (which has a wide range of meanings and implications). These challenges cannot be considered separately, and in combination, they become even more complex. Let's examine each more closely.

COMFORT

Have a seat in an uncomfortable chair. Soon you're squirming and fidgeting—if not actually in pain—and hoping to move on. That chair is not soon forgotten. Fortunately, most chairs fall into an area of passable comfort—not uncomfortable but not noticeably comfortable either. This is not surprising because comfort is a complicated issue, involving many variables. The biggest variable of all is the sitter. No one chair can possibly accommodate the wide range of height, weight, posture, musculature, and special needs and problems displayed by humanity. In one sense, comfortable chair design—or at least acceptably comfortable design—can be seen as an exercise in statistics. If nothing will work for everyone (a given), what will work for the majority of people?

One of the more intriguing aspects of chairmaking is the opportunity to custom design and fit the chair to the individual user—very different from the statistical approach. But this involves experimenting with the different variables that affect comfort. A few chairmakers have designed specially made fitting chairs that allow the sitter to try a wide range of dimensions, angles, and curves, which can then be used to design an actual chair (see the photo on the facing page). While this removes any doubt about dimensions and shapes, it can be a time-consuming and expensive approach. However, for those with problems finding comfortable chairs, this may be the only way. There are other, simpler—though less exact—ways to try out different ideas about comfort (see Chapter 3).

Another way to approach comfort is with the adjustable chair, now nearly ubiquitous in the workplace. With height, tilt, and back support all adjustable, very few people fall outside the range of acceptable comfort. Adjustable office chairs are usually not appropriate for dining rooms, however. Nor are they very good woodworking projects because molded plastic, welded steel, and gas cylinders are important elements in their design.

A really comfortable chair is a treasure, especially for the very large or small person. It is not impossible to find nor is it impossible to make. What makes a chair more than passably comfortable—comfortable enough to notice? It is not, as you might imagine, that the chair is completely custom-molded. People need to be free to shift around, change position easily, and keep circulation flowing in order to feel comfortable.

Function

This brings up another major variable in what makes a comfortable chair: function. How will the chair be used? Certainly, some chairs are used simply as decorative objects. Many look as if they were designed solely for that purpose in defiance of any practical use such as sitting. For the more pragmatically inclined, what one does in a chair makes an enormous difference in the perceived comfort. Read a novel in a dining chair? Type in an easy chair? Watch a movie in a task (secretarial) chair? None of these would be especially comfortable, regardless of how comfortable the chair feels when used for its intended purpose. So as a start, the design of the chair must match the use. Unfortunately, most chairs are used for a variety of activities. Dining chairs are used while eating, of course, but when the meal is over, people usually sit at the table and talk. They move their chairs back a little and settle into more relaxed positions. So a good design is one that allows for some flexibility of use.

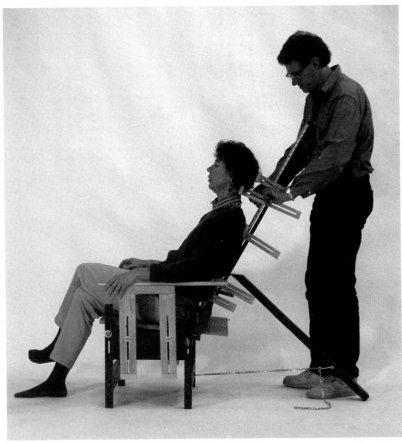

John and Caroline Grew-Sheridan can adjust for variations in dimension and shape with their specially made fitting chair. After setting up the chair for a comfortable fit, they can use the various parameters to design and make a custom chair. (Photo by Glenn Gordon.)

Dimensions

A chair's dimensions are an important part of comfort. There are no precise numbers, but there is a basic range of measurements relevant to the chairmaker. These will, at the very least, keep us away from making really uncomfortable chairs. (The dimensions that follow are mostly for dining chairs.)

The height at the front of the seat should be about 16½ in. to 17 in., although a range of 15 in. to 18 in. is acceptable for shorter or taller people as long as the dining table accommodates this as well. How should you take upholstery into account? The height should be estimated based on a compressed cushion. With the slip seats I use—normally 1⅜ in. to 1⅝ in. thick (cotton batting over foam)—the compression is

MATCHING ARMCHAIR AND NARROW-BACK SIDE CHAIR

To avoid awkwardly designed arms, make armchairs with wider backs to match narrow-backed chairs.

about 1 in. For materials other than foam, you may need to experiment a little, ask an upholsterer what to expect, or guess. The tolerances are fairly loose and not worth fretting over.

The depth of the seat should be roughly 15 in. to 18 in. Note that depth is measured from the front of the chair to the front of the chair's back. My dining chairs are usually 16 in. to 17 in. deep, which allows for a good range of motion and enough thigh support for most people. I've never heard a complaint that my chairs are too deep, but some taller people do find them shallow. The seat may be flat, or it may angle back as much as 4 degrees.

Seat width ranges from 16 in. to 22 in. (or even wider) but is normally around 18 in. to 20 in. Seats can and usually do taper toward the back. This can be a rather severe taper without adversely affecting comfort. My "Stained Glass Chair" (see the photo on p. 23) tapers from 20 in. at the front down to 9½ in. at the back over a 16-in. seat depth. Some people have mentioned that the chair looks as if it would not be comfortable, but all but one or two people who have been to my showroom over the last 10 years have found the chair very comfortable.

The space between the arms needs to be at least 19 in. and preferably 20 in. Spreading the arms farther apart than 22 in. may be uncomfortably wide. On chairs that taper toward the rear, it's important to leave enough room for the sitter's back between the arms (see the drawing at left). I place arms 7 in. to 8½ in. above the seat. But you should take into account the height of the table and its apron when designing or making armchairs. Smashing fingers between the arm of a chair and the table apron when scooting a chair in is not fun. Try to leave a 1½-in. gap.

For a much more thorough discussion of chair dimensions, consult *Humanscale 123* by N. Diffrient, A. Tilley, and J. Bardagjy (The MIT Press, 1974). This is an amazing set of cards with selector wheels that accompany a short book. *The Measure of Man* by H. Dreyfuss (Whitney Library of Design, 1967) is another good book on the subject. These books contain staggering amounts of information—fascinating or overwhelming, depending on your point of view.

Shape

Building a chair with appropriate dimensions will usually avoid real discomfort. But it's the angle and shape of the chair back that help to move the chair toward real comfort. For a dining chair, the back should be at approximately a 95-degree angle to the seat, but this is not easy to calculate if the back curves as well. I have experimented with different curves and have settled on a few variations—all similar to the basic shape, as shown in the drawing at right. I vary this shape to provide more or less lower back support. If you plan on making chairs with shaped backs, I strongly suggest that you play around with shapes, at least until you feel comfortable that a particular shape works for you. The dowel-chair project in Chapter 3 is an experiment with shapes and comfort and is a good place to begin.

The concave curve of the chair back—as on a horizontal slat—is another factor in the comfort of a chair and is not often considered. This curve creates a broader area of support for the back so that the back rests more on muscles than on the spine. I've used a wide variety of curves—with radii of anywhere from 18 in. to 60 in.—for different effects. Another design point that relates to the spine is to have an even number of slats on any slat-back chair (see Chapter 6). This allows the spine to rest comfortably between slats rather than directly on a slat.

DURABILITY

Chairs are subject to a lot of abuse in the course of normal usage. Simply sitting down on or standing up from a chair is a strain on it. Leaning into the back of the chair is a stress. Tipping back on the legs is an even greater stress. Chairs are scooted up to the table, dragged across the

POSSIBLE DESIGN FOR CURVE OF A CHAIR BACK (SIDE VIEW)

Scale: 1 square = 1 in.

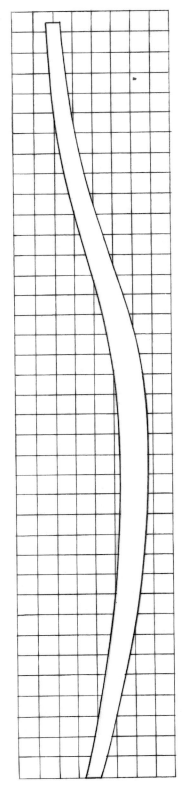

When sitting in a chair, the force tends to rack it backward.

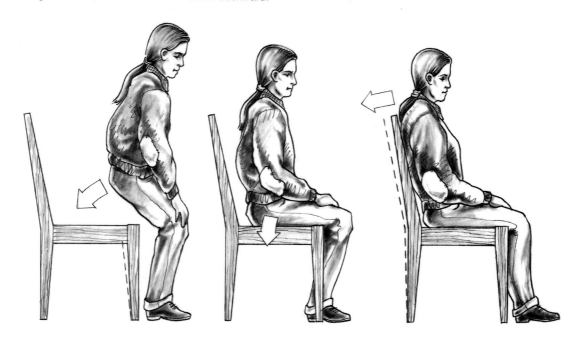

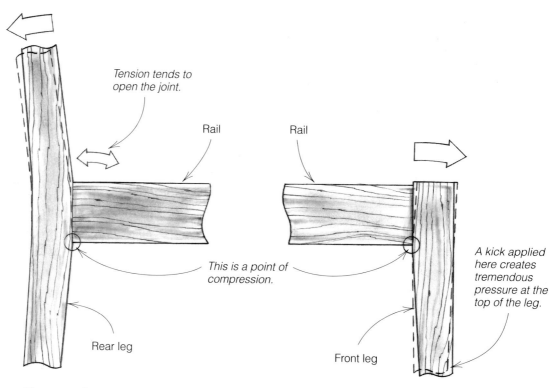

Tension tends to open the joint.

Rail

Rail

This is a point of compression.

A kick applied here creates tremendous pressure at the top of the leg.

Rear leg

Front leg

Close-up of rear-leg-to-rail joint

Close-up of front-leg-to-rail joint

floor, and used as step stools. And that's just by adults! My son used one of our store-bought chairs as a sort of walker, pushing it around in front of him until he broke one of the legs off. There are ample reasons for the demise of so many chairs; we ask a lot of them.

There are a number of factors that contribute to the durability of a chair. Joinery is foremost, but design elements such as stretchers and arms as well as wood use also play important roles.

Joinery

Most chairs fail at the joints between the side rails and the back. The dynamics of sitting mean that we plop down on the seat at an angle and then lean against the chair back. These motions put a great deal of stress on the joints, as the chair is first racked backward, then the upper part of the chair is forced back (see the drawing on the facing page). If this isn't bad enough, the length of the back gives a little extra

leverage to this stress. Most of this destructive force is applied to the joint between the seat and the back, although racking affects the front-leg-to-rail joints as well. There are other stresses, too. Scooting a chair back, pushing it around, or even kicking a leg applies a variety of forces to the bottom of the legs, forces that are magnified at the joints through leverage.

The way that one joins a chair is very important because the joinery is what holds the chair together. (The specifics of joinery will be discussed in greater detail in Chapter 2.) It is also important to reinforce the joinery by one or more methods. Corner blocks are most commonly used for reinforcement (as explained in the sidebar below), but other chair structures—such as stretchers and arms—also help.

Stretchers

Stretchers also contribute to the durability of a chair. When the legs are joined in an additional place (or

CORNER BLOCKS

Although not often seen as part of the chair's structure, corner blocks play an essential role in keeping the chair together (see the photo at right). They help to distribute all of the stresses along the rails and lessen strain on the joints themselves. They also serve as a second line of defense: Many a chair with failed joinery is held together with the corner blocks. The chair may feel loose, but at least it remains sittable until the corner blocks fail—and this can be a while.

Corner blocks can be attached with screws, sliding dovetails (a challenge that I'll leave for others), multiple tongue-and-groove joints, or even hanger bolts. Materials other than wood can be used for corner blocks, too. All function in the same way—to reinforce the joinery. Corner blocks also provide a place to attach the seat.

Corner blocks provide important reinforcement to the critical chair joints.

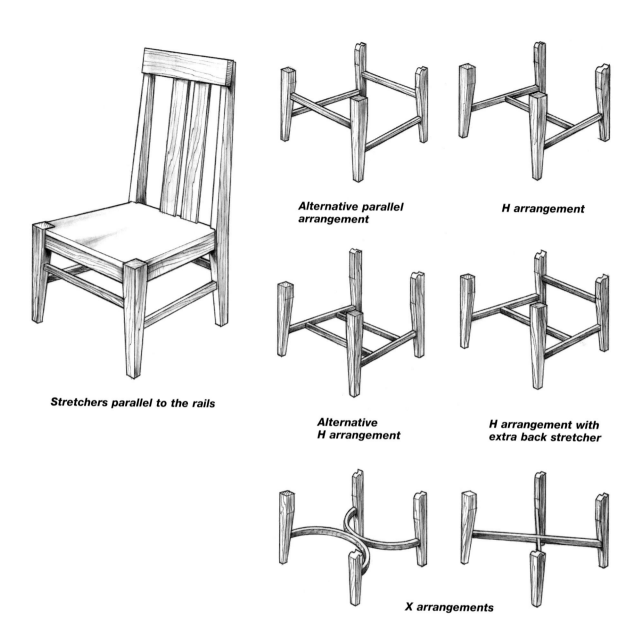

Stretchers parallel to the rails

Alternative parallel
arrangement

H arrangement

Alternative
H arrangement

H arrangement with
extra back stretcher

X arrangements

more places if double or triple stretchers are used), the whole structure is stiffened, and any force applied to one of the legs is shared with the others. Stretchers aren't usually connected to the legs with very significant joinery–frequently just a small mortise-and-tenon or dowel joint. Because of this, they don't work as well as back-up rein-

forcements like corner blocks, but they do help keep the chair together in the first place.

There are many possible arrangements for the stretchers (see the drawing above). The most effective structurally are those that parallel the rails, with front and side stretchers offset from each other so that the joinery doesn't interfere and weaken the leg. Multiple stretchers can be used in this arrangement. The lower the stretchers, the better they are structurally. But there are problems with this. Stretchers in the front get in the way of people tucking their legs under a chair or standing up, unless the stretchers are located high. Fortunately, the side-to-side stresses in a chair are not too serious, so locating the front and rear stretchers higher is not much of a compromise. Less effective structurally but better still at freeing up the front of the chair is the H arrangement: Side stretchers run from leg to leg and are connected by a center rung or two. An X arrangement of stretchers is interesting visually, but it is even less effective structurally because it only distributes diagonal forces against the legs and offers very little resistance to the more common forward and backward forces.

Arms

Arms also provide significant structural support to a chair, although this is true only for a particular type: arms that connect extended front legs with the back legs (see the drawing below). These arms strengthen a chair in the same way that stretchers do: They add another structural connection between the front and rear legs. Most arms that are attached in other ways don't add anything to the overall structural strength because they do not join the front and rear legs nor do they triangulate between the rear legs and the side rails effectively.

ARMS THAT HELP STRENGTHEN A CHAIR

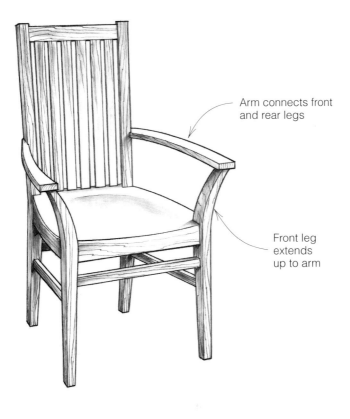

Arm connects front and rear legs

Front leg extends up to arm

Wood usage

In most circumstances, wood is a reliable structural element. However, ignoring the grain when cutting out chair parts can cause problems. The big issue is "run-out," or short grain. These are different names for basically the same situation—when the grain of the wood is angled across a part instead of running along its length (see the drawing below). Why is short grain weaker? The grain is a visual manifestation of the orientation of the wood fibers. Wood is much less susceptible to breakage across these fibers than it is between them. Try a simple experiment. Try to break a ¾-in. by 1-in. board with the grain running lengthwise. Then try to break a ¾-in. by 1-in. board (a cutoff from the end of a board, for example) with the grain running crosswise. You'll find that it's much easier to break the board with cross-wise grain. Avoid situations where your chair may have grain like this.

One place where this may not be obvious is at the bottom of the rear legs. If the legs are curved or angled back significantly, it is very easy to wind up with grain that runs out on an angle, leaving the back corner of the leg vulnerable. To minimize this, try to line up the curve of the leg with a natural curve in the grain. It is also possible to reduce the possibility of breakage by adding a glide to the bottom of the leg. This will keep the weak back corner off the floor and out of harm's way.

In critical situations where short grain is inevitable, it is better to consider bending the wood, either with steam or by lamination. This will maintain sound structure in parts that would otherwise be weak.

SHORT-GRAIN PROBLEMS

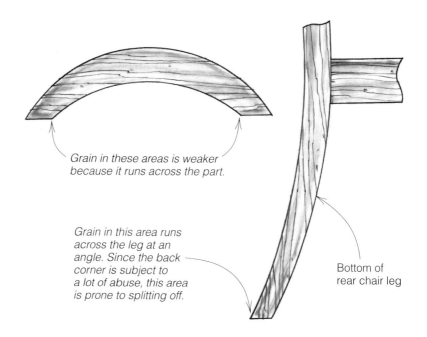

Grain in these areas is weaker because it runs across the part.

Grain in this area runs across the leg at an angle. Since the back corner is subject to a lot of abuse, this area is prone to splitting off.

Bottom of rear chair leg

The orientation of the grain also has an effect on the long-term life of the joints. The seasonal expansion and contraction of the wood is quite different depending on this grain orientation. But I think this is definitely secondary to good long-grain glue surfaces and well-fitted joints in providing durability to a chair. Considered strictly from the point of view of minimizing wood movement within a joint, the best orientation is to mortise in a flatsawn face of a board and to cut tenons in quartersawn rails. This is usually not practical or even possible. This is an example of when the best theoretical solution to a problem may not add enough to offset the problems it causes in other areas.

APPEARANCE

This is a topic far too big for this book. Rather than address the visual design of the chair, I will limit my discussion to the execution of a given design. And the biggest factor in this is how the wood is used.

Wood is incredibly varied in appearance, even within a species. The grain on different parts of the same board can be astonishingly different. Our goal is to use the wood in a visually unified manner. When picking out the wood for a chair or a set of chairs, we first must find wood that is basically similar in color and in grain. Once we have the necessary quantity of wood, we must decide what we want to use and where we want to use it. We want to create a visual design on the chair with a limited set of patterns—in other words, to paint with a palette of grain. How we cut and orient the wood will affect these results.

Most wood will show two distinctly different types of grain, depending on the orientation of the growth

rings relative to the surface. There is the straight, even grain (usually called quartersawn or riftsawn, depending on the angle) that we usually see when the growth rings are somewhere between 90 degrees (quartersawn) and 45 degrees (riftsawn) to the surface. And there is the more varied swirling or curving patterns (flatsawn) that we see when the growth rings are more nearly parallel to the surface (see the drawing at right). Since the growth rings curve and the surface of the wood is usually flat—at least to start—the grain on a wide board may change from straight to swirling and back to straight. A chair part cut from flat grain will show straight, quartersawn grain on edge (and vice versa). A part cut from grain that runs at roughly a 45-degree angle will usually show straight, riftsawn grain on all sides (see the drawing on p. 12).

What grain should you try for on a chair? The legs are an easy place to start because these are usually cut from thicker stock and are seen from four sides. They will normally be straight-grained. If possible, they should be cut from a board so that the end grain will run at about a 45-degree angle and the grain on all sides will be straight (see the drawing on p. 12).

With a curved leg, try to align the curve of the leg with any natural curve of the grain. You can try to cut the rails so that they show straight grain, too. The edges of a wider flatsawn board often have very straight grain. You could also cut quartersawn rails from thicker stock (12/4 would be necessary), but I rarely go that far. A balanced flatsawn grain pattern is fine, too, but try to avoid off-center and truncated patterns (see the photos on p. 13). If you're making a set of chairs, pay particular

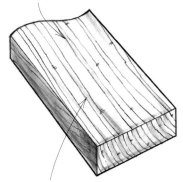

Straight grain
(quartersawn or riftsawn)

Quartersawn grain may show a high degree of figure (flecks and shimmer) in some woods.

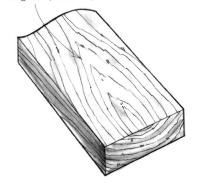

Swirling or curving pattern of grain (flatsawn)

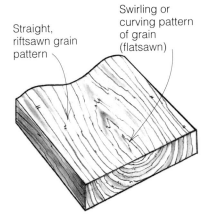

Straight, riftsawn grain pattern

Swirling or curving pattern of grain (flatsawn)

A wider board may display a variety of grain types.

GRAIN PATTERN ON LEGS

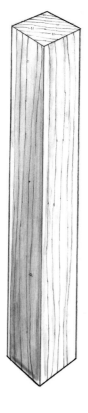

End grain that runs roughly from corner to corner yields a riftsawn grain pattern on all 4 sides of the leg—a uniform look that works very well.

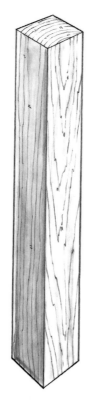

End grain that runs parallel to 2 sides will have straight grain on 2 sides and swirling grain on 2 sides. This is less uniform.

attention to the crest rails and the front and rear rails. From chair to chair, these should match quite closely in grain pattern. This will add a lot to the impact and unity of the set. It may not get much conscious attention, but it is one of the little details that add up to a significant overall impression.

Grain selection is a matter of taste. But it should be actively considered and not be just the result of random cutting and assembly. Don't think about grain choice as something that requires following a set of rules. The wood you have available will impose its own limitations and present its own opportunities. The more you know about grain, the greater your chance of getting good results.

DESIGN TRADE-OFFS

It should be apparent by now that the whole process of chair design is basically a series of trade-offs. This is not in any way limited or specific to chair design; trade-offs and compromises are at the heart of both woodworking and design. There is no ultimate solution to the problem of designing a chair. Even the best solutions are compromises. Comfort is always something of a compromise; structure often gets in the way of function or visual appeal. The appearance of a chair may be the most subjectively judged, but designing an attractive chair involves compromises of both structure and comfort. However, not all of the interplay between comfort, structure, and appearance involves major trade-offs. The elegant curve of a chair back may be comfortable and visually very pleasing. Some structural elements are striking visually and relatively comfortable as well. This is the stuff of the truly successful design—both rare and exciting.

Just because there isn't a definitive solution doesn't mean that some solutions aren't bad. When looked at dispassionately, a bad solution simply fails to solve the problems that the designer chose to address. Many chair designs ignore some of the basic rules, but usually this is so that some other basic rule can be followed or some specific goal attained. Some chairs are so comfortable that we forgive less than stunning appearance. Some chairs are so interesting to look at that we forgive the lack of structure, comfort, or even both. People may find the attractive yet virtually unsittable pieces ridiculous as chairs. But as mentioned earlier, chairs are more than just things to sit on.

Above left: Straight grain on both the front rail and the crest rail looks good and is easy to carry through in a complete set of chairs.

Above right: Symmetrical flatsawn grain works well, too, but it will be harder to make all of the chairs in a set match.

Left: Asymmetrical grain on the rails is clearly not a disaster, but it is nicer, especially in sets, to exercise more care in choosing the wood.

A GALLERY OF CHAIRS

How we sit and what we sit on are very personal and very revealing. Chairs support us both physically and metaphorically. They assist us in our posture and in our posturing.

Chairs have been important in many cultures throughout recorded history. Drawings and actual examples of sophisticated chairs survive from ancient Egypt. These come from the tombs of high dignitaries, who were buried with objects of great importance. But chairs evolved from both "low" and "high" forms—from the strictly utilitarian (in those cultures that didn't sit on the floor and therefore considered chairs necessary) and the highly ceremonial. There were different types of design at work. In one case, designs evolved based on practical, functional concerns, not the least of which was cost. In the other case, design was based on style, impact, and image. Chairs that were not strictly utilitarian were originally the domain of the powerful and were very strong symbols of that power. In many settings, the only chairs present were for the powerful.

The connection between chairs and power is still very much alive, although it is much more subtle. Office chairs are a good example. The secretarial chair and the executive chair are quite different in looks and function, and thus in the message they send. And the more important the executive, the higher, wider, and taller the chair back is. Chairs help to convey authority in a language of cultural symbolism.

Even our language reveals some very interesting associations between chairs and power, chairs and positions of authority, and chairs and status. A powerful set of meanings and metaphors have grown up around the word and the object, which is a direct result of the historical associations between chairs and power. As a verb, "to chair" means "to occupy the place of authority." The "chairman" is the leader of a group (because the leader was the one who originally sat). The candidate runs for a seat in Congress or a seat in Parliament. In court, one approaches the bench. At a university, the professor hopes to wind up with an endowed chair—a secure and prestigious position. All of this for a place to rest our bottoms!

The following chairs are some of my classic and contemporary favorites. I chose some to illustrate more fully realized examples of the chair projects in this book. Some reflect the design evolution from "low" forms: the Shaker and Windsor chairs and Brian Boggs's fan-back chair, for example. Others demonstrate the great variety in chairs with "high" lineage: from the Chinese yoke-back armchair to the "Millenium 3" chair by John Makepeace. These are clearly important chairs for important people. Some were designed to further ideals of simplicity: the Stickley chair, the Shaker chairs, and the Nakashima chair, for example. Others, such as the Mackintosh and the Phyfe chairs, were designed for more opulent settings. Some are obviously comfortable. Some are clearly not. But all of these chairs reflect the variety of creative approaches to the problems of chair design.

Shaker side chairs. Circa 1840, Enfield, Connecticut.
Part of what makes these Shaker chairs so effective is the detailing and proportioning. The use of wood is exquisite. (Private collection. Photo by Jim Strong, Inc., New York.)

A fan-back chair by Brian Boggs.
A chair with contemporary elegance, this chair is still firmly rooted in the rustic Appalachian tradition of chairmaking. (Photo by Scott Phillips.)

**Continuous-arm and sack-back
Windsor chairs by Michael
Dunbar.**
Two fine examples of contemporary
Windsor chairs. (Photos by Andrew
Edgar.)

Yoke-back armchairs (Chinese).
A matched pair of very refined and beautifully detailed chairs. The wood is huanghuali with pine seat boards and a cane seat. Late Ming or early Qing dynasty, 17th century. (Gift of American Friends of China, 1947.528 with 1947.529. Photo by Robert Hashimoto. © 1996, The Art Institute of Chicago. All rights reserved.)

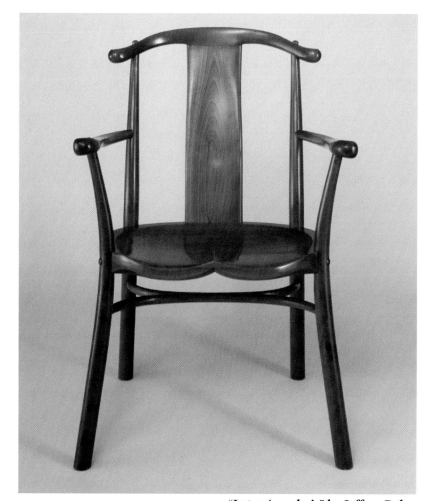

A dining room chair by Frank Lloyd Wright.
This striking chair was designed for use around a dining table. The high backs of the chairs around the table created a peaceful inner space for Wright's family, removed from those serving the meal. Servants were important, however, because if someone didn't hold the chair as one got up from the table, it could easily fall over. (Photo courtesy the Frank Lloyd Wright Home and Studio Foundation.)

"Lotus Armchair" by Jeffrey Dale.
This is heavily influenced by traditional Chinese chairs, but the structure is quite different. It is more closely related to the carved-seat chairs with the legs attached to the outside of the seat plank with screws. (Photo by Jeffrey Dale.)

Gustav Stickley. No. 1350 1904–1905.
Right angles, but the back angles back and the slats curve, adding to the comfort. (Photo courtesy Vitra Design Museum Collection, Weil am Rhein, Germany.)

A side chair by George Grant Elmslie (American, 1871–1952). Circa 1910.
Beautiful ornamentation based loosely on classical trefoil distinguishes this chair. Oak and leather. (Mrs. William P. Boggess II Fund, 1973.342. Photo © 1996, The Art Institute of Chicago. All rights reserved.)

High-backed armchair by Charles Rennie Mackintosh.
Originally designed for the Argyle Street Tea Rooms. A simple structure turned into a unique and elegant design through the bold use of form. (Photo © Hunterian Art Gallery, University of Glasgow, Scotland, Mackintosh Collection.)

Michael Thonet & Sohne. No. 14 1859–1860.
Thonet & Sohne were masters of steam bending. This chair has two steam-bent hoops to which all of the other parts (also steam-bent) attach. Gebruder Thonet was the first large-scale manufacturer of chairs. (Photo courtesy Vitra Design Museum Collection, Weil am Rhein, Germany.)

Armchair by Curtis Erpelding.
This elegant chair has a laminated
apron and also laminated front legs
and arms. This makes for a very
strong chair and adds to the
refinement. Note the beautiful detail
work. (Photo by Curtis Erpelding.)

Josef Hoffmann. No. 728 1905.
A classic of modern café chairs.
(Photo courtesy Vitra Design Museum
Collection, Weil am Rhein, Germany.)

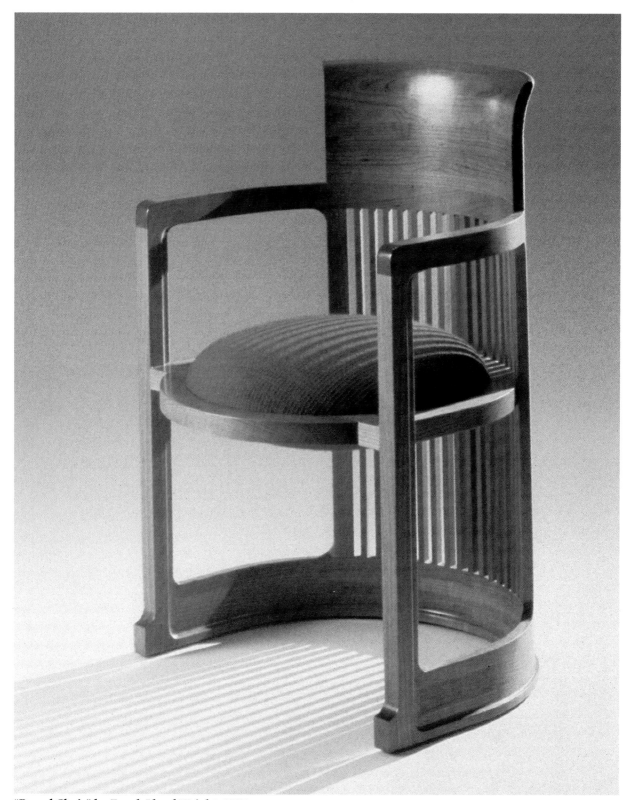

"Barrel Chair" by Frank Lloyd Wright. 1937.
A very cohesive design from which little can be taken away without completely
destroying the whole of the design. (Photo courtesy Cassina USA.)

"Stained Glass Chair" by Jeff Miller. 1990.
The back dominates this chair with its comfortable curve and the ebonized walnut inlays in the style of window leading. (Photo by Stuart Block.)

"Spider Chair" by Jeff Miller. 1993.
A very animated chair. The legs are each cut from a single piece of wood. (Photo by Tanya Tucka.)

Lyre-back side chair by Duncan Phyfe. 1810–1820.
Beautifully designed and highly detailed. This is 1 of a set of 13 chairs. These chairs are the culmination of the neo-Grecian style. (Photo courtesy The Metropolitan Museum of Art, gift of the family of Mr. and Mrs. Andrew Varick Stout, in their memory, 1965.) (65.188.2.)

"C/Y" side chair by Carolyn and John Grew-Sheridan.
This is a contemporary version of an 1810 Duncan Phyfe side chair. The lyre is laminated and provides a comfortable and durable back support. The lyres on the originals were neither. (Photo by Schopplein Studio.)

Low-back armchair by Sam Maloof.
Maloof's style is very much his own with the distinctive shaping and the mastery of the "hard edge" created by the intersection of curved surfaces. (Photo by Gene Sasse, Inc.)

"Circle-Back Chair" by Gregg Lipton.
A distinctive and playful graphic style with the circle of the back mirrored in the hollowing of the seat. (Photo by Stretch.)

"van Muyden" chairs by Robert Erickson.
The sweeping comfortable curve of the back support and rear leg (a bent lamination) is also the central visual element in these chairs. (Photo by Steve Solinsky.)

"Conoid Chair" by George Nakashima (American, 1905–1990). 1988.
An intriguing combination of a cantilevered construction with elements of a Windsor chair. Walnut with hickory. (Raymond W. Garbe Fund in honor of Carl A. Erickson, Sr., 1988.204. Photo by Robert Hashimoto. © 1996, The Art Institute of Chicago. All rights reserved.)

"Millenium 3 Chair" by John Makepeace (Dorset, England, 1939−). 1988.
This is one of my favorite chairs. An awesome technical feat entirely at the
service of a beautiful, organic chair. The chair is commanding yet peaceful.
English holly wood. (Restricted gift of an anonymous donor, 1990.578 frontal.
Photo by Robert Hashimoto. © 1996, The Art Institute of Chicago. All rights
reserved.)

Alvar Aalto. No. 31 1931.
A laminated cantilever is the
dominant element in this design.
(Photo courtesy Vitra Design Museum
Collection, Weil am Rhein, Germany.)

**"Zig Zag Chair" by Gerrit T.
Reitveld. 1934.**
A strikingly simple solid wood
cantilever. Made of solid elm with
mitered, splined, and reinforced
joints below and a dovetailed back.
(Photo courtesy Vitra Design Museum
Collection, Weil am Rhein, Germany.)

**"The Chair" by Hans Wegner.
(1949 JH501).**
This classic chair is beautiful in its
purity. The shaping and joining of
arms and back is quite complex,
however. (Photo courtesy Vitra
Design Museum Collection, Weil am
Rhein, Germany.)

**"Stack-Back Armchair" by Robert
De Fuccio.**
The back is a stack lamination, and
the seat and rear legs are steam bent
on this café-style chair. (Photo
courtesy Thonet.)

2

CHAIRMAKING BASICS

Once you have settled on a design for a chair, you have to decide how to execute the design. In truth, this is still part of the design process but is more concrete in nature: You need to decide which joinery to use and how to cut it, and you need to decide how to shape the various parts of the chair. As you will see, these factors are closely related to each other.

JOINERY OPTIONS

The joinery on a chair is critical to its health and survival. With so many options available for putting a chair together, it is important to consider the strengths and weaknesses of each. Basically, a good joint requires a strong mechanical fit, with the parts physically locked together or held together with a significant amount of friction, or good long-grain-to-long-grain glue surfaces—or a combination of the two.

To complicate matters, almost all joinery between perpendicular pieces of wood is affected by the expansion and contraction of the wood as it cycles through periods of humidity and dryness (see the drawing on the facing page). What this means is that all joints are subject to some movement and stress with just the change of seasons. Compression of the wood is another factor that contributes to loosening joints when they are subject to as much abuse as they are on a chair. The forces that rack a chair can cause enough pressure to compress wood fibers and thus loosen the joints.

There are three types of joints commonly used in chairmaking: dowel joints, mortise-and-tenon or mortise-and-floating-tenon joints, and various hardware joinery. Let's examine each type.

The dowel joint

Dowels, especially when used in pairs (also referred to as double dowels), are very common in mass-produced chairs (see the photo on the facing page). With the right machinery, doweling is very fast, accurate, and easily repeatable. There are automatic dowel-hole-boring machines, glue injectors, automatic dowel inserters, dowels with premeasured glue "pods" that automatically dispense the glue, and numerous jigs for the home shop. All of this for a joint that has some serious limitations! Dowels make a reasonably

WOOD MOVEMENT AS AFFECTED
BY CHANGES IN MOISTURE CONTENT

Wood movement in flatsawn and quartersawn boards

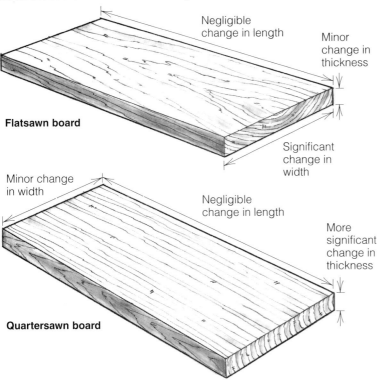

Flatsawn board

Negligible
change in length

Minor
change in
thickness

Significant
change in
width

Minor change
in width

Negligible
change in length

More
significant
change in
thickness

Quartersawn board

Wood movement in a typical mortise-and-tenon joint

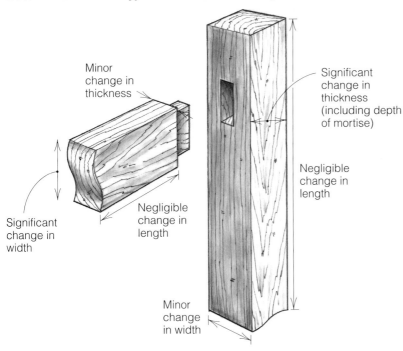

Minor
change in
thickness

Significant
change in
width

Negligible
change in
length

Significant
change in
thickness
(including depth
of mortise)

Negligible
change in
length

Minor
change
in width

**A dowel joint with two ⅜-in.
dowels is what you will find in
most mass-produced chairs.**

The mortise and tenon is a better chair joint than a dowel joint. This is an example of a routed mortise. The ends of the tenon were rounded over to fit.

strong joint when the parts are only subject to shearing force (a force perpendicular to the dowels). They are of questionable durability when there is either racking force or withdrawal force (forces that pull the pieces apart in line with the dowels) at work, and both of these are significant in chairs.

Since a dowel joint does not physically lock together the parts being joined, the most important factor in its success as a joint is the long-grain-to-long-grain glue surface. A dowel in a hole drilled into end grain—such as at the end of a chair rail—will have the entire circumference of the hole as a good glue surface. But inserted into a hole drilled in long grain—such as in the leg to which the rail will be attached—there are only two points on the sides of the hole that are truly long grain. Everything else is tending toward end grain, which does not contribute significantly to glued-joint strength. Seasonal wood move-

ment also works to break the glue joint. This may explain why so many doweled chairs come apart. So why is the dowel joint so favored by industry? Because it is fast, easy, and accurate. Corner blocks help to strengthen dowel joints, allowing a chair to stay together long enough to be acceptable to industry. However, there are better joints for chairmaking.

The mortise-and-tenon joint
The mortise-and-tenon joint has been the classic furniture joint for centuries (see the photo at left). It offers excellent mechanical strength and good long-grain glue surface. A good fit is critical to the joint's strength, however, and this is not nearly as easy to achieve as with a dowel joint.

Working with mortise-and-tenon joints involves careful planning. There are many different things to take into account when laying out, cutting, and fitting the joint. For example, how thick should a tenon or a mortise be? As a rule of thumb, a mortise or tenon should be roughly one-third to one-half the thickness of the board in which it is cut. In determining both length and width (and thickness) of the mortise or tenon, we want to maximize the glue surface but minimize weakening the parts. So a mortise or tenon should be as wide as possible but also should not come too close to the top of a leg, or the leg may easily split. Length for a tenon, or depth for a mortise, is most often limited by how close the intersection of two joints is.

Another consideration is if it is acceptable to have the mortises intersect. A leg with two joints at the top is definitely weakened by having the mortises intersect. But joints in the leg are usually strengthened with

Cutaway of a leg with mortises that don't intersect

Cutaway of a leg with intersecting mortises (tenons will have to be mitered)

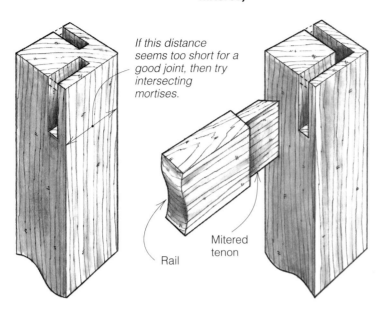

If this distance seems too short for a good joint, then try intersecting mortises.

Rail

Mitered tenon

longer (intersecting) mortise-and-tenon joints because there is more glue surface available. I try not to intersect the joints but sometimes I do so I can have longer tenons and therefore more glue surface (see the drawing above). This brings up another consideration: locating the joint. Although it is easier to cut a centered mortise-and-tenon joint on the workpiece, I rarely do that because there are some clear advantages to having the joint off-center. On chairs (and any other piece of furniture where the situation is similar), there is room for longer tenons the farther the joint is located to the outside of the leg. Obviously there is a limit. I usually leave ¼ in. to 5⁄16 in. so I don't weaken the leg much.

There is much debate about whether you should square the ends of routed mortises or round the ends of the tenons to match the mortise. There are reasons for both. Chop-

ping the ends of the mortises square gives you a little bit more long-grain glue surface. Rounding over the edges of the tenons is often faster, especially since some machines cut rounded tenons. The differences are not significant enough to worry about, at least not in relation to the other variables. Use whichever method you are more comfortable with.

Fitting the joint is one of the most important aspects of a good mortise-and-tenon joint. I always cut mortises first because the tenons are much easier to fit to the mortises than vice versa. Then comes test cutting the tenon. Even with a carefully and accurately made jig, you will wind up with some variation in fit. Different woods cut differently, template guides are not always concentric, and so on. As a double check, I take a scrap—preferably a cutoff of the same rail stock I will ultimately use—and cut a test tenon. The goal is to

The shoulder plane is made for jobs like fitting tenons. Plane across the grain, and be careful not to round over the tenon cheeks.

achieve a fit tight enough to put together by hand, but with some effort. If the test tenon is too small, I'll adjust my jig accordingly. Once I'm as close as I can get or as close as patience allows, I'll cut the real joints. If they inexplicably come out loose, I will just glue on a patch and proceed as for a tight joint. If they're tight, it's time to fit by hand. My first choice for this is a shoulder plane. It takes some practice to cut evenly across the tenon (see the photo above). Take a swipe or two across the tenon, then test the fit again. You can alternate sides of the tenon so you don't change the location, or you can remove the wood from one side if you need to correct a slightly mislocated tenon.

You can also use a rasp or sandpaper on a block to size tenons. These are simpler than using a shoulder plane, but they have drawbacks. Neither will get right down to the shoulder

of the tenon, so that will have to be cleaned up afterward with a chisel. There is also a tendency to round over the surface of the tenon a little, reducing the glue surface and loosening the mechanical fit.

The major difference between the regular mortise-and-tenon joint and the floating or loose version is that on a floating tenon, matching mortises are cut in both parts to be joined. Then a separate tenon is made to fit the mortises (see the left photo on the facing page). The main advantage of the floating tenon is that there are no real tenons to cut. All parts are cut to exact size, with the appropriate angles on the ends of rails, slats, and so on. The main disadvantage is that cutting mortises on the ends of rails requires some specialized equipment or jigs.

All difficulties aside, the mortise and tenon is still the best joint for chair-

The mortise-and-floating-tenon joint is a good substitute for the mortise and tenon, especially where cutting a tenon is difficult. First mortise both sides of the joint. Then mill up long strips of the tenon stock, and cut the lengths you need.

This example of a bolted joint has a barrel nut drilled into the rail. The dowels keep the parts from rotating.

making. Later in this chapter, I will discuss ways to make cutting both mortises and tenons easier, faster, and more trouble-free.

Hardware joinery

By now, you've probably figured out that I prefer wood-to-wood joinery. But that doesn't mean that I don't use hardware where appropriate. Screws, bolts and nuts (including barrel nuts and T-nuts), and even some types of knockdown fittings have legitimate, although specialized places in chairmaking (see the right photo above). They join certain types of arms, attach corner blocks and seats, and even join an apron to a leg on certain types of chairs.

Screws are very effective for attaching pieces together, but only in the right circumstances. Screws do not work well in end grain. The wood fibers tend to shear off between the screw threads, allowing the screw to pull out. Screwing long-grain surfaces together works well, especially in combination with glue. But even here, the combination of seasonal expansion and contraction with repeated stress can weaken the glue joint and cause the wood around the screw to compress, leaving a hole that is too large to hold the screw securely and therefore a loose (or failed) joint.

It might appear that a bolted joint is the answer because there is no glue to fail and the joint seems likely to remain tight forever if the bolt itself doesn't loosen. But this isn't the case. Unfortunately, if the bolt and nut are the primary means of holding the parts together, the compressibility of wood and the normal expansion and contraction work to loosen the joint. As the joint is stressed and/or as the wood absorbs moisture and expands against the fixed length of the bolt, some of the wood fibers will be compressed. In drier weather, when the wood dries out and contracts, the joint may loosen. And the loosening can permit racking, which causes more compression. The simplest solution is to allow for tightening every so often. But this brings up the problem of visibility. With any hardware, unless it is a part of the design (and it certainly can be) or hidden (as in the café chair in Chapter 8), the holes need to be plugged. And if they are plugged, retightening is impossible.

The bottom line is that hardware may not be appropriate for a wide range of chairs, but it is effective and appropriate in the specialized situations referred to or on chairs like the captain's chair in Chapter 9, where the hardware works in conjunction with the joinery.

SHAPING OPTIONS

The other major issue in executing a chair design is shaping the chair parts. This wouldn't be all that bad, except that there are joints in the shaped parts—joints that must be located accurately. In this way, shaping and joinery are linked, and the two need to be considered together. This is a little different from how you may approach other projects like tables or cabinets. There are two

---

AN EXPERIMENT WITH CORNER BLOCKS

All of the joints in chairmaking have strong points, and all have problems. As with chair design, there is no perfect solution. Fortunately, all joints can be strengthened with corner blocks.

I've experimented with the power of corner blocks by building a chair with unglued dowel joints. First I tried sitting in the chair without any reinforcement. Since unglued dowels do not hold in any significant way, the chair was very wobbly and quite unsafe. I then screwed corner blocks into place to see what would change. The chair felt surprisingly solid at first but loosened up considerably over time. However, the chair is still together and still safe to sit on. This may be why dowels are good enough for industry: The corner blocks allow for a reasonable time (reasonable for industry, that is) to pass before failure. This is why I prefer mortise-and-tenon joints. There is redundancy. The mortise-and-tenon joints and the corner blocks reinforce each other. This allows for an even more reasonable time before failure—especially for a chairmaker who has better things to do than to work on a piece more than once.

Corner blocks are an essential element in chair durability. Note that at least four screws are necessary to help reinforce the joinery.

strategies I use to address the specific problems of shaping and joining chair parts: cutting the joints before or after shaping.

The first is simple: Cut the joints in square stock, then cut out the desired shape. The advantage to working this way is that it makes it much easier to cut the joints when working with the stock before it has shape. However, this usually means using a thicker or wider board than necessary—in other words, wasting wood. This can be a small price to pay for easier joinery. Once you start working on sets of chairs, however, you may want to take advantage of efficiencies that preclude cutting the joints first.

The other option is to shape the parts first, then cut the joinery. This can use the wood more efficiently. But cutting the joinery must be carefully planned out or even jigged up before beginning. When working with preshaped parts, you need to imagine the part as if it were still encased in a square board, then work out a way to hold it in this position for cutting the joints. In other words, the concept of cutting joints in square stock is still relevant. I usually do more than just imagine; I cut joints in square stock when I'm working out the design on a prototype. Then, when I switch to building a run of chairs, I use the parts from the prototype (or the cutoffs) to make jigs to hold the shaped parts in place for the joinery operations (see the drawing at right).

THE SHAPING PROCESS

Shaping chair parts is usually a two-step process: cutting the parts to shape and then smoothing them so that all surfaces are ready for finishing. When there are many identical

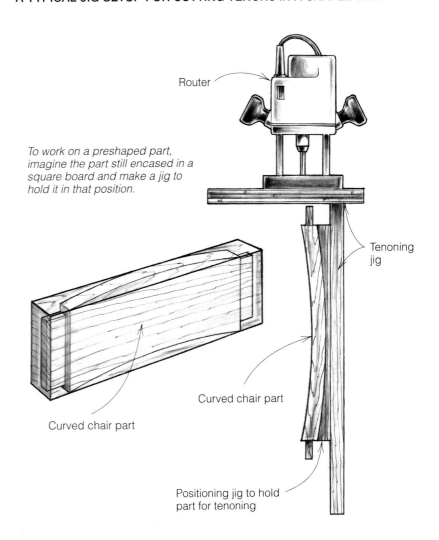

A TYPICAL JIG SETUP FOR CUTTING TENONS IN A SHAPED PART

Router

To work on a preshaped part, imagine the part still encased in a square board and make a jig to hold it in that position.

Tenoning jig

Curved chair part

Curved chair part

Positioning jig to hold part for tenoning

parts, a third step—flush-trimming—is sometimes added between rough cutting and smoothing in order to shape more consistently and to get closer to a finished surface.

Cutting to shape

The primary tool I use for shaping parts from solid stock is the bandsaw. Other alternatives exist, such as the scroll saw or bowsaw, but they have limitations. For one chair, you might be able to put up with anything. But for more than one, it will probably pay to seek out a bandsaw.

Careful layout comes first, then locating and cutting all the joinery, if that is appropriate. Then the part is bandsawn to shape. Keep to the waste side of the line, but the closer to the line you can stay, the less work will be necessary later.

Smoothing

Getting from a bandsawn curve to a finished surface is a task best approached with a variety of different methods.

Smoothing with planes. The straight sections are easy. Hand planing with a smooth or jack plane can work quickly and beautifully. If the bandsawn cut is not very even, sometimes I will start with the jointer if the part is of adequate size and shape to be safely handled. Then I'll move back to the hand plane.

To a limited extent, planing with a smooth plane will also work on gentle convex or concave curves. Gentle concave curves can be planed by holding the plane at a steep angle, which will effectively shorten the length of the plane's sole. A compass plane is a tool specifically designed to cut both convex and concave curves and is adjustable to many different curves. I use this tool often. A spokeshave will also work on

FLUSH TRIMMING

Flush trimming is sometimes used as an interim step between rough cutting and smoothing, especially if there are a lot of identically shaped parts to cut and smooth. There are many variations on the basic concept of trimming parts flush to a pattern. A variety of tools can be used in different situations and with different results.

The bandsaw can be set up to saw out roughly duplicate parts. First make a simple wooden guide bar with a notch on one end for the bandsaw blade and enough clearance underneath for the workpiece. Angle the bar so that you can easily clamp it in place. Then attach the pattern to the workpiece and cut, holding the pattern against the bar. If this is set up just right, you can then flush-trim on the router with the same pattern in place.

A router can also be used for trimming roughly shaped parts that are not too thick. This is usually done on a router table with a flush-trimming bit. Flush-trimming bits come with bearings either above or below the cutter. Both types are useful.

Flush trimming on the bandsaw

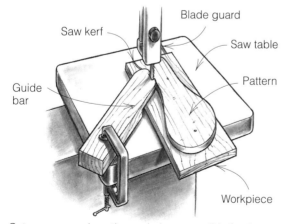

Guide bar
Saw kerf
Blade guard
Saw table
Pattern
Workpiece

Cut away enough so the workpiece can slide freely underneath. The bar must contact the pattern.

Flush-trimming bits

Bearing
Cutter

Bit with bearing above the cutter

Cutter
Bearing

Bit with bearing below the cutter

curves, but with its short sole, it usually follows irregularities rather than eliminates them. Holding the spokeshave at an angle can help because this effectively lengthens the spokeshave's sole.

A sharp plane can leave an unrivaled surface, but only if the grain allows. If the grain is uncooperative and changes direction, the result can be less than satisfying.

Smoothing with scrapers. Scraping is the next alternative because scraping is not usually affected by the direction of the grain. Scraping is slower work than planing, and it tends to burn the thumbs. (Try to find leather thumb guards, which are available through carving suppliers and are great for this.) A scraped surface is not quite as nice as a planed one. And the scraper (like a spokeshave) has a tendency to follow rather than eliminate irregularities. Holding the scraper on an angle can keep it from falling into every ripple, but it still may not smooth a fair curve.

Smoothing with sandpaper. Sanding has advantages and disadvantages, not unlike planing and scraping. I list it last because I usually resort to it last, after trying plan-

You can nail a pattern to the top of a roughly shaped part and use it with a bit with the bearing under the cutter (in the router table, the bearing will be on top). A combined pattern and workpiece holder can also be used with a bit with the bearing above the cutter. The edge of the pattern rides against the bearing and guides the bit.

Even the tablesaw can be used to flush-trim parts (as long as the cuts are straight). An L-shaped flush-trimming jig for the tablesaw is simple to make and use. Be aware that short cutoffs accumulating under the jig can bind and shoot out from underneath at high speed. So be sure to stop the saw regularly to clear out all cutoffs frequently.

Flush trimming on the router table

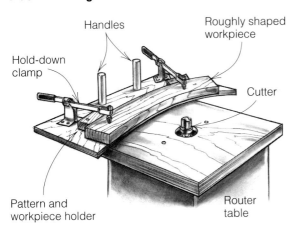

Handles

Roughly shaped workpiece

Hold-down clamp

Cutter

Pattern and workpiece holder

Router table

Flush trimming on the tablesaw

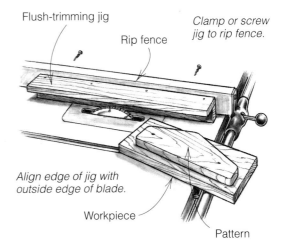

Flush-trimming jig

Clamp or screw jig to rip fence.

Rip fence

Align edge of jig with outside edge of blade.

Workpiece

Pattern

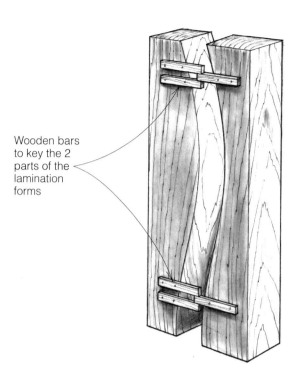

Wooden bars
to key the 2
parts of the
lamination
forms

Strip laminating a chair slat requires carefully made forms and a lot of clamps. Lining up the pencil marks aligns the forms in this example.

ing, then scraping. Hand sanding is a slow and messy method for smoothing, and it is prone to rounding over surfaces. Machine sanding isn't slow, but it is messier and is even more prone to rounding over if not destroying parts altogether. But sanding has some major advantages, too. It can smooth regardless of problems with the grain. It can be used to fair a curve with the help of a properly shaped sanding block. And it is much easier than planing or scraping, both of which require sharp and well-tuned tools and a high degree of skill.

Other methods for shaping wood

There are a few other ways to shape wood, which are designed to get around the problems that can arise when shaping solid stock.

Lamination. Another method that I use is lamination. Lamination is a technique that opens up many design possibilities that would otherwise be impractical or impossible. Lamination can be done in two ways: by gluing thin strips together around a form or by stacking and gluing larger pieces together—usually like bricks—and then cutting to shape. (See the "Stack-Back Armchair" on p. 29.) Cutting and shaping are ultimately like working with solid stock, as discussed above. In both cases, great strength is achieved. A laminated curve is stronger than a similarly shaped piece cut from solid wood because the solid piece would likely be weakened by grain running across a narrow section. Strip lamination is actually stronger than a similarly sized straight piece of wood. It also allows

A vacuum press is ideal for gluing up strip-laminated parts. This cuts in half the amount of form making and eliminates the need for countless clamps.

great freedom of shape while retaining structural integrity. (See the "Millenium 3 Chair" on p. 27 and the Aalto chair on p. 28.)

Strip lamination requires forms on which the work is bent and clamped to shape. Usually, there need to be both male and female forms, with ways to ensure correct alignment when they are clamped together around the glued-up strips (see the photo and drawing on the facing page). This can be as elaborate as wooden bars that slide together or as simple as penciled registration marks. However, it is also possible to do strip laminations in a vacuum press, which can eliminate one of the forms and all of the clamps (see the photo above).

As with solid wood shaping, it is important to plan out the joinery for strip-laminated parts in advance. Often, the forms themselves can be a big help in holding parts in position for the sake of cutting the joints. Or a section of the form can be copied to make a jig for holding the part for joinery. In certain situations, it may be necessary to figure out the joinery later—after a portion of the chair is assembled. This commonly occurs on strip-laminated slats for the back of a chair; determining the exact angle of the tenons must wait until the back of the chair is dry-assembled.

Strip lamination requires many thin layers of wood. Thick veneer ($\frac{1}{16}$ in. to $\frac{1}{10}$ in.) can be used, or the wood can be sawn into strips from a solid board (see the photo on p. 42). Whether to use veneer or strips

Ripping strips of wood for strip
lamination should always be
done to the outside of the blade.
This means resetting the saw
fence with each cut, but it's a
small price to pay for safety. Note
the layout triangle, which helps
to keep the strips in order.

There are a few problems with this
method. The process of bending
with steam causes some wood fibers
to stretch and others to compress.
This weakens the pieces a little,
sometimes enough to cause breakage during the bending process. The
use of a fixed length bending strap
(or compression strap) can significantly reduce breakage. Steam-bent
pieces often "unbend" some when
taken out of the form after drying.
The precise amount of this spring-
back is hard to determine in advance, and the results can vary from
piece to piece. This is why I tend to
rely on lamination for curved chair
parts on my joined chairs instead of
steam bending.

CHAIRMAKING JIGS

To make your chairmaking substan-
tially easier and more precise, there
are a few jigs you should consider
building. These jigs are designed to
simplify and speed up some of the
more challenging aspects of making
a chair: mortising, tenoning, and leveling chair legs. (There are many other jigs specific to individual chairs,
and these will be discussed in the appropriate chapters.)

Mortising jigs

There are two methods that I use to
cut mortises with a plunge router:
using a mortising block and using
mortising templates. The first is a
way to hold the workpiece and stabi-
lize the router while working. The
second method uses templates and a
guide bushing, sometimes called a
template guide, in the router to locate the cut.

The mortising block. In router
mortising you need a way to help
support and guide the router on a
narrow piece while it is cutting. The
support can be as simple as a piece
of wood the same thickness as the

sawn from solid stock is usually de-
cided on the basis of the width of
strips needed, the availability of
good veneer, and one's tolerance for
lots of ripping. If you're cutting your
own, it helps to use the thickest
strips that will comfortably bend to
the smallest radius required. There
will be fewer strips, less glue to deal
with, and less cutting.

Steam bending. Although you can
create similar shapes, bending with
steam is an entirely different process
than bending by lamination. Steam
bending is an integral part of certain
types of chair construction (see the
Windsor chairs on p. 16 and the
Thonet chair on p. 20). Steam—or
heat and moisture—causes the fibers
in wood to become more elastic. In
many woods, this flexibility is
enough to allow significant bending.
In other woods, little bending is possible. If the wood is bent, clamped in
a form, and then allowed to dry, the
bent shape is basically retained.

BUILDING A MORTISING BLOCK

A very simple yet flexible approach to mortising is to make a mortising block—a block of wood roughly 3½ in. by 3¼ in. by 30 in. (one piece or glued up) for use with a router. To keep the router fence tight against the block, I add a wooden auxiliary fence to my router fence.

I made this auxiliary fence wide enough to extend below the actual router fence. Then I screwed a spacer block the same thickness as the auxiliary fence (and sized so as not to interfere with it) to the bottom of the back side of the block. I added a couple of pieces of paper as shims, then screwed a full-length guide strip to the spacer blocks. The guide strip is wide enough to hold the auxiliary fence against the block.

For greater flexibility, I also drilled six different holes in the mortising block for the hold-downs clamping the workpiece to the block.

To use the mortising block, clamp the leg to be mortised to the block flush with the top. The router fence rides on the far side of the block. Rout the mortise in a series of shallow passes.

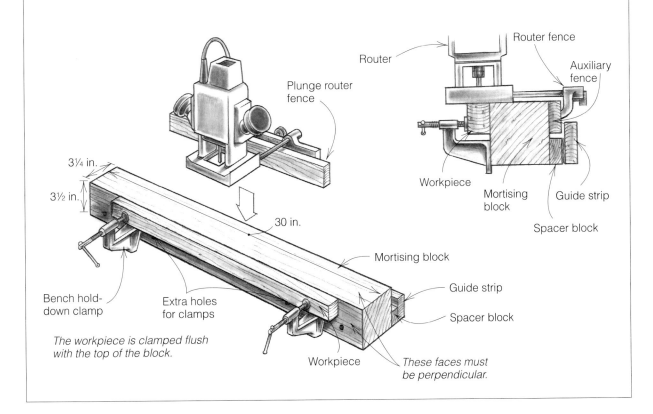

Plunge router fence

Router

Router fence

Auxiliary fence

Workpiece

Mortising block

Guide strip

Spacer block

3¼ in.

3½ in.

30 in.

Mortising block

Guide strip

Spacer block

Bench hold-down clamp

Extra holes for clamps

Workpiece

The workpiece is clamped flush with the top of the block.

These faces must be perpendicular.

USING A MORTISING TEMPLATE

I made this mortising template for cutting mortises in curved parts. It is best used in conjunction with a custom fence, which positions the template accurately. The template is a simple rectangle of wood with a hole in it in the shape of a mortise. The template hole can be routed or drilled and carefully filed or sanded to shape. The sides need to be straight and parallel. Once you've made one, you can use a flush-trimming router bit to copy it. (Note: You will need a fence/template combination for each side of the chair and each mortise.)

To calculate the size of the template hole, start with the desired mortise size. Add to this the difference between the diameter of the router bit and the diameter of the guide bushing. For example: a ⅜-in. by 2-in. mortise with a ¼-in. bit and a ⅝-in. guide bushing would yield a template hole ¾ in. by 2⅜ in. (⅜ in. + [⅝ in. − ¼ in.] = ¾ in.; 2 in. + [⅝ in. − ¼ in.] = 2⅜ in.

To use the template, first trace one side and the end of the workpiece onto a ¾-in. scrap, then cut out the fence. Lay out the exact mortise location on the work-piece. Holding the fence in position, place the opening in the template in position over the mortise location. Clamp the fence and template together, then attach them with screws. Clamp in place on the workpiece and rout the mortise.

This precisely located mortise in the curved rear leg of a chair is a perfect example of mortising with a template.

Mortising template

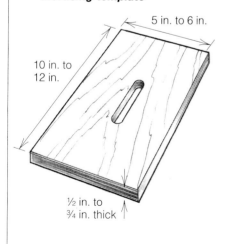

5 in. to 6 in.

10 in. to 12 in.

½ in. to ¾ in. thick

Using a mortising template

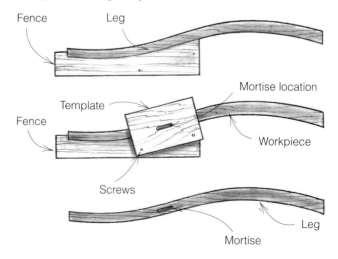

Fence

Leg

Fence

Template

Mortise location

Workpiece

Screws

Mortise

Leg

part being mortised, or it can even be an identical part clamped appropriately next to the workpiece. The router fence attachment then guides the router. These solutions work but are awkward to use. I have made up a mortising block that is very versatile, quick to set up, and easy to use (see the sidebar on p. 43). The workpiece is clamped flush with the top of the block. The side-to-side mortise location is controlled by the router fence riding against the block, and the mortise length is controlled by routing only to the marked lines. For situations where there are many similarly sized mortises to cut, you can even clamp or screw stops into place to limit the router travel and control the mortise size. This is a very simple way to cut mortises, especially for those averse to using jigs. I used this setup for most of the projects in this book.

The mortising template. Using a mortising template is a different approach to the same problem. It is very consistent and very simple to use (see the sidebar on the facing page).

The templates are made of ½-in.- to ¾-in.-thick material; plywood, solid wood, acrylic, and aluminum all work. A slot with round ends is cut in the middle of the plate, sized so that the router, fitted with a guide bushing and a bit, will cut the exact-size mortise required. The plates can be simply positioned and clamped to a workpiece. But the real advantage comes when attaching a part-specific fence, which locates the mortise repeatably and accurately. This is terrific for cutting mortises on the flat sides of curved parts.

To cut the mortise, a series of shallow passes are taken until the mortise depth is reached. Be careful that

the bit is fully enclosed by the guide bushing and locked in this position, when you try to lift up or set down the router while it is running.

Tenoning jigs

There are many tenoning jigs available for the tablesaw. All of them have the same problem: It takes an extra setup or two to cut the shoulders. It's also hard to keep the shoulders even all the way around the tenon.

I prefer to cut tenons with a plunge router and a shopmade tenoning jig. This cuts the cheeks and the shoulders at the same time—clean, square, and well aligned. It is also very easy to cut angled tenons with the jig by attaching a wedge. See the sidebar on pp. 46-47 for how to make and use the jig.

Chair-leg leveling jigs

Leveling the four legs of a chair is such a source of anxiety that there are jokes (bad ones, of course) about attempting to level the legs and ending up with a chair an inch or two off the floor. In truth, it isn't all that hard to level a chair (or a table for that matter) if you're slow and methodical.

The most reliable way I've found to level the legs on a chair is to use a shopmade jig (see the top photo on p. 48). It's just a simple leveling table that's used in conjunction with a handsaw with no set to the teeth (such as a Japanese kugihki, often referred to as a flush-cutting saw). Start with a 24-in.- to 30-in.-square piece of medium-density fiberboard (MDF). (You can use plywood, but it's usually not as flat.) Rout a very shallow recess in one corner exactly the depth of the saw thickness, and then a deeper hole in the recess for the long leg. Set the chair on the leveling jig with three legs resting on

MAKING AND USING A ROUTER TENONING JIG

This tenoning jig for the router is quite simple to make and use. The workpiece support holds the part to be tenoned upright and positions the router so you can cut the tenon on the end of the part. The tenoning template guides the cuts. The router—fitted with a guide bushing and a straight bit—follows a guide strip to cut the tenon, first on one side of the strip, then on the other. The location of the tenon can be controlled by where you position the tenoning template on top of the horizontal platform on the workpiece support. You can use clamps, screws, or bolts and T-nuts to secure the template.

Start by making the workpiece support (see the drawing on the facing page). I used Baltic birch plywood, although any stable material should work. Cut a dado in the horizontal platform to help attach it to the main upright of the workpice support, then attach braces. Cut or rout the opening in the horizontal platform. Then add a spacer block (this gives the router some room to work without cutting into the jig) and a fence. Be sure the fence is at a right angle to the horizontal platform.

To make the tenoning template, rip a 7-in. by 14-in. by ¾-in.-thick board down the middle, then cut a 1-in. by 4-in. notch in each half to form the opening that will be on either side of a guide strip. Glue the two halves to a ¼-in. by ¾-in.-thick guide strip. Make this strip from maple for stiffness. (You will have to make different-size templates in different situations.)

You need to align the guide strip so that it will guide the cut parallel to the edge of a workpiece. To do this, clamp a ¾-in.-thick by 3½-in.-wide reference board to the workpiece support so that it extends through the opening in the horizontal platform. Then place the tenoning template so the guide strip is lined up exactly with this board, and clamp the template to the horizontal platform. Attach two ¾-in. by 1-in. runners to the bottom of the template, so that they fit tightly to the horizontal platform. These runners keep the template aligned if you move it to adjust for tenon position. Remove the reference board.

To use the template, clamp your workpiece to the workpiece support with an edge against the fence and the top flush with the bottom of the tenoning template. Locate the template where you want to cut the tenon, and clamp or screw into place. Set the plunge router depth of cut to control the tenon length.

To use the tenoning jig, clamp it in the vise, and clamp the workpiece to the jig, with the top resting against the tenoning template.

Place the router on the tenoning template in its upright and locked position. Turn the router on, then plunge down to the full depth of cut. Cut with many light passes until the side of the tenon is completey cut, then raise the router and shut it down. When the router stops, shift over to the opening on the other side of the guide strip and finish cutting the tenon.

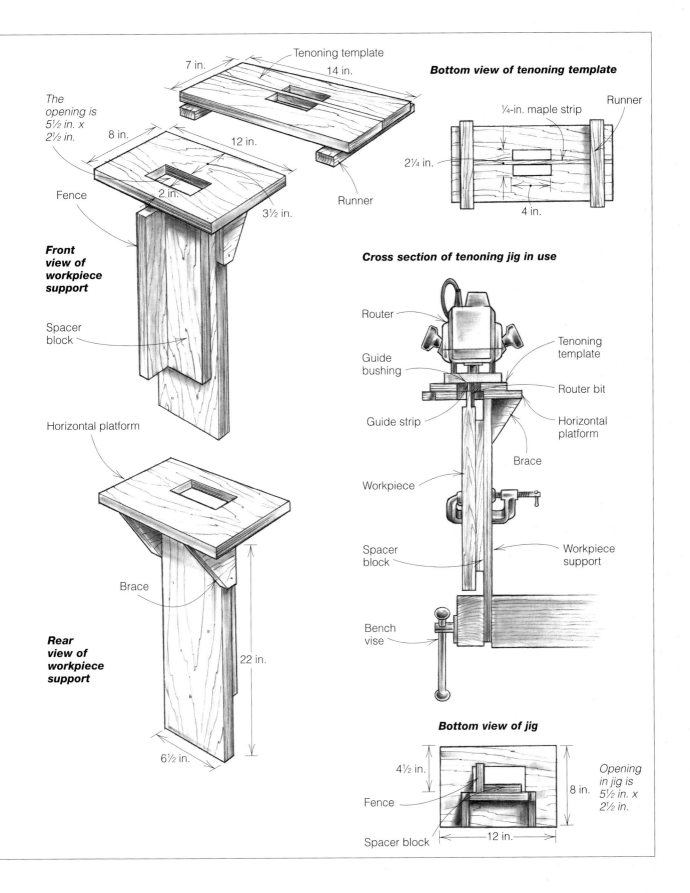

Tenoning template

7 in.

14 in.

The opening is 5½ in. x 2½ in.

8 in.

12 in.

2 in.

3½ in.

Runner

Fence

Front view of workpiece support

Spacer block

Bottom view of tenoning template

Runner

¼-in. maple strip

2¼ in.

4 in.

Cross section of tenoning jig in use

Router

Guide bushing

Guide strip

Workpiece

Spacer block

Bench vise

Tenoning template

Router bit

Horizontal platform

Brace

Workpiece support

Horizontal platform

Brace

Rear view of workpiece support

22 in.

6½ in.

Bottom view of jig

4½ in.

8 in.

Fence

Spacer block

12 in.

Opening in jig is 5½ in. x 2½ in.

Cutting the long leg with the chair-leg leveler is reliable and easy.

surface. I use either my saw table or the top of my 16-in. jointer. A piece of ¾-in. or 1-in.-thick medium-density fiberboard (MDF) about 24 in. to 30 in. square also works well. For a minor wobble, I will usually just sand down one of the long legs. I put a piece of 100-grit sandpaper on the saw table, and pull it out from under one of the offending legs a number of times while holding the leg steady with the other hand. If you prefer, you could tape the sandpaper down and rub the leg on it. Either way, be careful not to let another leg fall off the table while you're concentrating on leveling, or you'll be doing more than just a little sanding to make everything right.

Which leg is the offending one? It's either of the two that rest on the level surface when the chair wobbles back and forth. I usually measure to be sure the distance from the legs to the bottom of the rail is consistent, but I'm not sure it really matters that much. If you're in doubt after measuring—and this is often the case—simply split the difference and sand some off both long legs. (Make

the surface and the long leg in the hole. Then clamp a handscrew (or just a block of wood) to the long leg to keep the chair from tipping into the hole. I've actually attached my handscrew to the jig's surface so that the chair is held both level and secure for cutting. Keeping the saw flat on the shallow recess, trim the long leg exactly flush with the rest of the surface.

Other leveling options. If making the leveling jig seems like too much work, try these low-tech options. The key to leveling a chair is a flat

A chair-leg leveler is not always necessary. To accurately mark the leg you need to cut, scribe the long leg level with the surface on which the other legs are resting. Then cut or sand the leg to the scribed line.

sure to chamfer the bottom of the leg slightly, so you don't split off a section when you sand.)

If it appears the problem is bigger than you can fix with a little bit of sanding, try this: Hang one of the long legs off the side of the flat surface so that the other three legs rest evenly. Scribe a knife line even with the surface, and then cut or sand to this line (see the bottom photo on the facing page).

MAKING A SET OF CHAIRS

All of these jigs will help significantly if you decide to make a set of chairs. But there is one more bit of advice before you start: Buy enough wood. Buy sufficient wood to make extra parts and maybe even enough to make an extra chair to allow for a slipup or two or for a hidden blem-

ish in the wood. And if you wind up with the extra chair, you can always find a use for it. (What a great gift it would make!) Having extra wood means you can select what you want rather than scramble to get what you need. And if you've picked wood carefully for matching grain and you run out, it may be very difficult to find a piece to fit in well with the rest.

Organization becomes an issue as well. Keeping track of what goes where can be a surprising challenge when parts are literally all over the place. You will need to be very careful to mark parts, joints (if they are not interchangeable), and orientations, or you will run into some very frustrating problems. There are no special techniques I can offer to deal with this other than the admonition to start and stay more organized than usual.

A big set of 50 chairs is almost ready to go out the door in my old shop. Toward the end, the biggest problem was just moving everything around.

3
DOWEL CHAIR

This chair project is different from all that follow. The dowel chair is actually four different projects: two studies in dimensions, comfort, and curves; and two versions of a simple chair with minimal joinery. The most significant lessons to be learned here are about the curves that provide comfort in a chair. But it is also fun to make such a comfortable chair with relatively little work.

A dowel chair looks as if it would never work. Dowels that are ³⁄₈ in. or ¹⁄₂ in. in diameter don't appear to form a likely structure for a chair, but with the dowels closely spaced, the sitter's weight is well distributed, and they are strong enough. I have already discussed why dowel joints (or round tenons) do not make especially good joints (see p. 30). So why bother with a chair that uses these joints? Put enough of them together—35 or so—and they create a structure sturdy enough to hold up to the abuses a chair is subject to. I built my first version of this chair 10 years ago, knocking it together out of scrap plywood and a bunch of hardware-store dowels (see the left photo on p. 52). I didn't even bother to glue it together because it was only intended to test the comfort of a curve. However, it served as my lunch chair for years. I also enjoyed demonstrating its strength by standing on the seat for amazed visitors. I'm not sure if they were more amazed by the chair or my antics.

MAKING TWO STUDY CHAIRS

There are a lot of ways to test out chair designs—some crude, some sophisticated, and some overly elaborate. I tend to stick to the crude so I can get the answers I need quickly, and then move on. A dowel chair is one of the fastest ways to try out different curves and dimensions.

It is even possible to make an adjustable dowel chair, although it can only adjust on a grid, creating very rough approximations of the curves you need. Still, this can provide enough feedback on which to base some dimensional decisions. And more refined testing is also very quick. Is it necessary to build an adjustable dowel chair? Not really because the basic dimensions and

The author's original dowel chair is 10 years old and still together—still comfortable, too—even though it wasn't glued.

The adjustable dowel chair is not bad-looking in an odd sort of way. I wouldn't put it in my living room, however.

curves are given in this book. But I use this simple project to help answer questions that come up from time to time in chairmaking.

An adjustable dowel chair

The first step in creating an adjustable dowel chair is to build two side pieces out of 2x4s (see the drawing on the facing page for dimensions). Mine are screwed together with drywall screws. Attach some ½-in. hardware cloth (available at hardware stores) to the sides of the frames with screws and washers or staples. Then attach two cross-pieces to the backs of the frames, leaving 16½ in. to 17 in. between them. Insert 35 to 40 dowels—⅜ in.

or preferably ⁷⁄₁₆ in. (if you can find them)—to create a seat and a back (see the right photo above). You can't create real curves because you're working with a fairly large grid on the hardware cloth, but you can get an approximation. Start at the front of the seat, and make it about 17 in. high. Then set up the "chair" with the seat and the back at right angles to each other. Now you can play around. One caution with this chair: It's not as sturdy as any of the other versions of the dowel chair. The dowels are supported only at two points, and this provides less resistance to flex in the dowels. Sit down and stand up gently—and don't try to stand on the dowels.

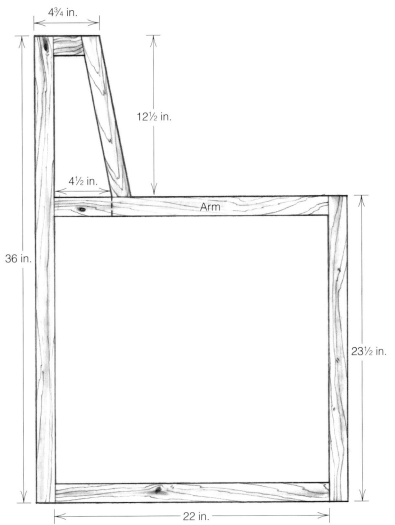

Build the side frames with 2x4 lumber.

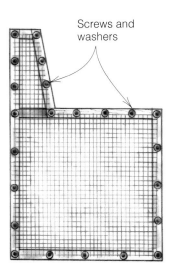

Attach the hardware cloth with screws and washers or staples.

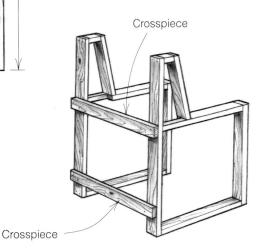

Attach the crosspieces to the back with two screws at each joint (the hardware cloth is not shown for clarity).

With this in mind, try the chair out. How short a seat is too short? What about too deep? Try lowering the front edge of the seat to create a more comfortable "curve" for the backs of the legs.

Now experiment with curves for the back. You will quickly run into one of the limitations of this chair. It's hard to get a true test of curves. If you find a profile that seems promising and you would like to refine it further, draw the rough curve full size on graph paper, then smooth out all of the bumps. It's time to move on to the next study chair.

A test chair

This chair is perfect for learning more about comfortable curves. It's a quick, no-nonsense project that provides excellent feedback. This is the same as my original scrap plywood chair—two pieces of plywood with holes drilled for the dowels. To begin, I suggest you use my profile as a starting point and play with it a little. Or you can test out one of your own. Later in this chapter, I'll discuss ways to do this, but you should try anything that seems to work.

To start, cut two pieces of plywood to rough size, according to the dimensions in the drawing at left. Then, lay out the chair profile full size and at the proper location on one of the pieces of plywood. To enlarge one of the scale drawings, mark out a grid of 1-in. squares on the plywood or, if you prefer, on a sheet of paper that you can staple or tape to the plywood. Working from the scale drawing, enlarge the shape of the seat profile square by square.

Next, mark out the centers for the dowel holes. Use a set of dividers (essentially a compass with two points instead of a point and a pencil) that are set to about 1¼ in. between points if you're using ½-in. dowels, or 1 in. to 1⅛ in. between points if you're using ⅜-in. or ⁷/₁₆-in. dowels. "Walk" the dividers up the seat profile line, marking where the holes will be drilled (see the photo on the facing page). Tack or screw both

A BASIC SHAPE FOR PLYWOOD SIDES FOR THE TEST CHAIR
Scale: 1 square = 1 in.

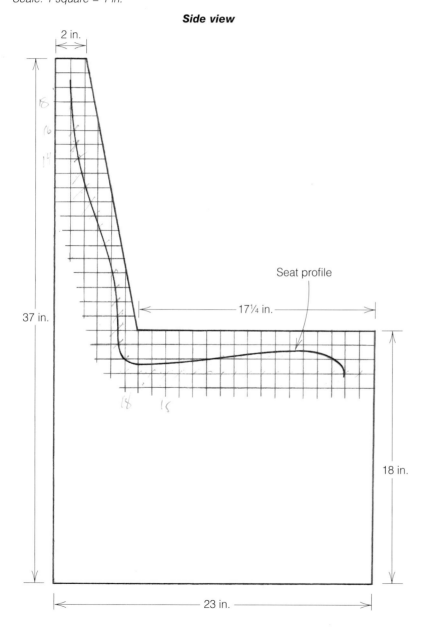

Side view

pieces of plywood together in preparation for drilling.

Now it's time to drill. A drill press is ideal if you have one. However, you will need to clamp a board to the drill press table to support the chair as you drill (see the photo on p. 56). Drilling with a portable drill stand also works, although it's not as precise. Drilling by hand is possible, but the inevitable variations from perpendicular will make it harder to assemble the chair and will add some bends to the dowels that will affect the comfort. With a hand drill, you'll also need to make a depth stop. This doesn't need to be anything more than a small block of wood sized to prevent drilling deeper than desired. Drill a hole through it, and leave the stop on the drill bit. Drill through the marked plywood side and most of the way through the other, attached side.

Assembly is next. How do you get 35 dowels into both sides of the chair? Start by tapping all of the dowels into the holes that don't go through the side. Then place the side with through holes on the workbench with the inside of the chair facing up. Invert the side with the dowels, and insert the dowel at the front edge of the seat into its corresponding hole. You will have to hold the upper side at an angle to do this, allowing you to work on the dowels one at a time. Tap the first dowel down into its hole a little with a mallet. Then line up the next dowel with its hole. You should be able to push most of the dowels in by hand or with gentle tapping. Keep lining up the next dowel, or two or three, then tap them down to seat them better. When you've gotten all of the dowels in their holes, tap or pound the side down until the dowels are flush with the side.

Using dividers to mark the dowel hole spacing is quicker, easier, and more accurate than measuring and marking with a ruler.

DOWELS AND HOLES — PART 1

You've amassed a pile of ⅜-in., ⁷⁄₁₆-in., or ½-in. dowels for your study chair. What size are they really, though? Dowels are rarely sized exactly, and even if they were cut and sanded perfectly round and precisely to the stated size, normal expansion and contraction of the wood would probably change the size a little and make them slightly oval. For a study chair, ease of assembly is important. You should try to drill your holes just slightly larger than the dowels. Fortunately, most hardware-store dowels are a little bit undersized. Drill a test hole in a scrap of wood, and try out the fit. You should be able to insert the dowel without too much effort. If you have to pound it in or if it is loose enough to drop in with no effort, try a different drill bit. Different types of bits will often drill slightly different-size holes. If my brad point drill isn't right, I'll try a spade bit, a Forstner, or a twist drill. I've occasionally used metric, letter, or other fractionally sized drills when necessary.

Drilling the holes in the two plywood sides requires a clamped-on support table for the drill press.

The chair will probably be a little wobbly. Don't worry about the strength. If you want to stiffen up the side-to-side wobble, just clamp or screw a board between the sides. The real issue is the comfort of the curve, and this chair should be comfortable. If you find a small area that you don't like, you might be able to get away with removing some dowels while the chair is still together, plugging the holes using lengths of dowel and glue, and, after the glue has dried, drilling again. Otherwise you'll have to knock the whole chair apart. You can use the same piece of plywood, and drill a whole new set of holes if you shift the pattern over so the new holes fall roughly halfway between the original ones. The point of this exercise is to find out for yourself what is comfortable—to create a curve that works for you.

Developing your own seat profile

How do you come up with your own profile? I suggest a few approaches: Adapt (or copy, as a nondesigner might say) something else you like, fool around with the adjustable chair, or draw a curve from someone's back.

The first approach is the most reliable. The chair you're adapting exists and can be tested for comfort. The adjustable dowel chair has limitations that we discussed previously, but it can still be a good start. Drawing a curve directly off someone's (or your own) back is most useful for a fairly erect sitting posture. It is almost impossible to sit in a relaxed posture without existing support. I used this method to make the typing chair I'm sitting in to write this book. I glued a pencil into a hole in the end of a 24-in.-long ⅝-in. dowel to transfer the curve of my back to a piece of plywood at my side. Drawing your own curve is best done with an assistant, but you can add a handle to the dowel and pencil to mark your back without contorting too much in the process (see the photo at right). This is only a start, though. When I first tried the chair that I marked this way, it felt too short in the seat. I extended the seat length, which helped a little, but the chair still felt wrong. It occurred to me that seat length wasn't the real problem; the lower back seemed too far forward. I changed the shape of the lower back to give it more room, and that helped the seat depth and the comfort of the back. There was still a place that hit me wrong in the upper back, so I marked the offending dowel and reworked the curve to relocate that dowel and the ones around it. Uncomfortable fit is almost never the result of just one dowel, unless one is significantly out of line. Usually, several have to be adjusted to achieve a smooth curve.

Test your chair out in different settings. Is it as comfortable for typing as it is for eating or for reading a book? Think a little bit about how you sit for different activities over the course of a day. Does this help your understanding of comfort and function? Try increasing or decreasing the lumbar support, or tipping the chair back a bit more (try tacking a block of wood or a chair glide to the front or back) to see what effects these changes have in different situations. And live with the chair for awhile to see if your impressions change. Once you're comfortable with your chair profile, it's time to make a piece of furniture.

MAKING A REAL DOWEL CHAIR

Once you have a curve that you like, you can use it to make an actual chair. You have two options for the sides: solid wood or plywood. With

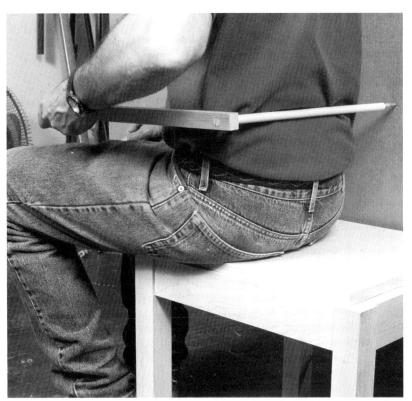

The author marks his own back profile for a typing chair.

solid sides, there is some joinery involved. With plywood, joinery is eliminated, but you have to glue up a double thickness of plywood for strength. Neither version is difficult.

For either side option, begin by making a chair pattern (see the drawing on p. 58). Enlarge the drawing onto a piece of ¼-in. plywood. Transfer the seat profile as well. If you are using your own seat profile for the chair, start by enlarging my drawing to get a general idea of the chair's shape. You may have to modify the rear leg a little so that the profile stays roughly centered. Don't try for exactly centered. Instead, try to create a flowing, pleasing curve to the leg. Mark off the dowel center locations with dividers, a compass, or a ruler, and drill small (³⁄₃₂-in.) holes through the pattern at each dowel location. I used ½-in. dowels for this chair, spaced 1¼ in. on center.

PATTERN FOR THE DOWEL CHAIR
Scale: 1 square = 1 in.

Side view

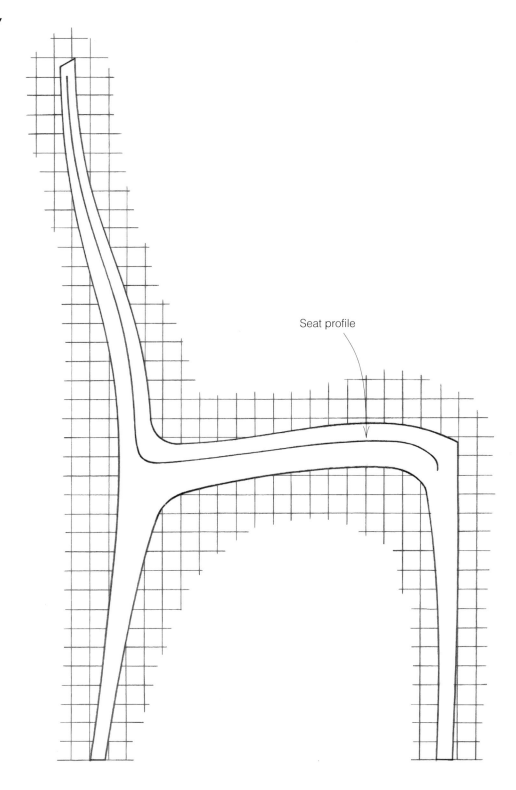

Seat profile

Using solid wood for sides

If you are making a solid wood dowel chair, take a few moments to plan out the joinery before you cut out the pattern. The drawing at right shows the way the three boards join together and the appropriate dimensions for my version of the chair. If you've opted to use your own seat profile, check if this will work for you. Draw three rectangles to contain the rear leg, seat rail, and front leg, then verify that the chair pattern fits inside the rectangles and that the joints between parts are in the appropriate places (roughly in the middle of the transition curves).

Now choose the wood for the chair sides. Ideally, you should attempt to get all of the wood for the chair out of one board or a pair of matched boards. Try to orient the grain for the legs so that the grain goes diagonally from the outside back corner to the inside front corner on the tops of both front and rear legs (see the drawing on p. 60). This is not always possible.

If you have access to a planer, plane the wood to 1⅜ in. Otherwise, go with 6/4 surfaced lumber (1¼ in. thick) from the lumberyard. Cut the front and rear legs to the dimensions of the rectangles you drew above. For the seat rail, however, you need to add length for the half-lap joints that extend through the legs and hold the sides together. The seat rail comes all the way through to the front of the front leg. At the rear leg, you only need to add enough length to reach the back of the leg to be cut—3¹⁄₁₆ in. on my version—not the full 5 in. of the rectangular blank.

Before you start cutting the half-lap joints, look at your wood once again to make sure that you are cutting in the right place and using the best grain orientation (refer again to the

JOINERY FOR THE SOLID WOOD DOWEL CHAIR

The chair side is made up of three rectangular boards. This shows basically how it should fit in those rectangles. These are the actual dimensions for the rectangles on my chair. (Your chair may be different.)

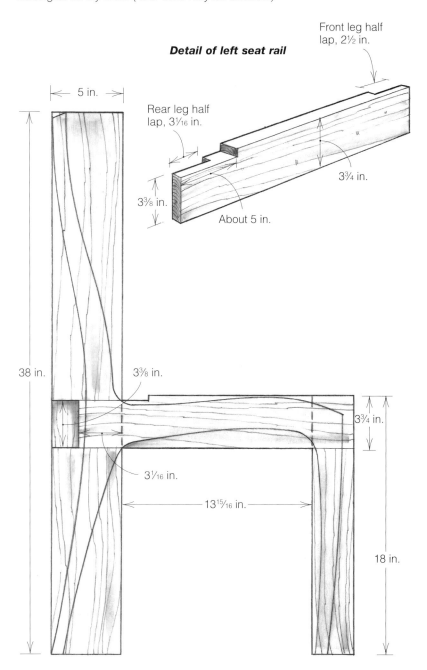

Detail of left seat rail

Front leg half lap, 2½ in.

Rear leg half lap, 3¹⁄₁₆ in.

3¾ in.

3⅜ in.

About 5 in.

5 in.

38 in.

3⅜ in.

3¹⁄₁₆ in.

3¾ in.

13¹⁵⁄₁₆ in.

18 in.

IDEAL GRAIN ORIENTATION FOR REAR LEGS

Rear leg on rear leg blank

Ideally, the end grain should be on a diagonal from outside rear corner to inside front corner.

Front view of dowel chair

Notice how the grain is balanced.

drawing above). Remember that there is a left and a right side to the chair and that they are different. Making two lefts or rights is an easy way to start a pair of chairs, but this tends to double the time you'll put into the project. On the rear legs, you'll have to carefully locate both sides of the half lap. Note that this joint is not the full 3¾-in. width of the seat rail but is only 3⅜ in. wide. This enables you to cut right-angle joints and still have a seat that curves up gently toward the front.

Once the lap is cut on the back of the seat rail, cut the top of the rail down to fit the rear leg joint. I like to do this as a stop cut on the tablesaw. Cut in about 4 in., then hold the workpiece tightly against the fence

and the table and shut down the saw. Don't move anything until the blade has stopped moving. Then cut away the waste on the bandsaw.

Dry-fit the side pieces together, and make sure everything lines up. If you haven't already done so, cut out the chair pattern, smooth it carefully, and trace the pattern onto the dry-assembled parts. Make sure you have a left and a right side to the chair. Cut the parts to shape, and smooth them while they are still separate pieces, except for the areas around the transition curves. You can leave these curves and some of the final shaping and sanding until after the side pieces are assembled. I also like to taper the inside faces of the front and rear legs down to 1 in. thick at the bottoms and also to the same thickness at the top of the rear legs. The tapers are not necessary, but they add to the grace of the chair. If desired, mark out the tapers on the edges, then bandsaw to outside of the line. Clean up the cuts with a hand plane. (Make sure you keep the tapers away from the half-lap joints.)

Now glue and clamp the chair pieces together, making sure the shoulders of the half laps stay tight. Once the glue has dried, do a final smoothing, and mark out the locations for the holes on the inside faces. (You'll need to mark from both sides of the pattern.) Then profile the edges with a ⅜-in. roundover bit in a router.

Using plywood for sides
I originally thought that a plywood chair would be easier to make than the solid-wood version. There is no joinery at all to worry about. But to get the necessary thickness, you do have to glue two layers of plywood together, and smoothing the edges is not as easy as it is with solid wood.

NESTING SIDES FOR ECONOMICAL USE OF PLYWOOD

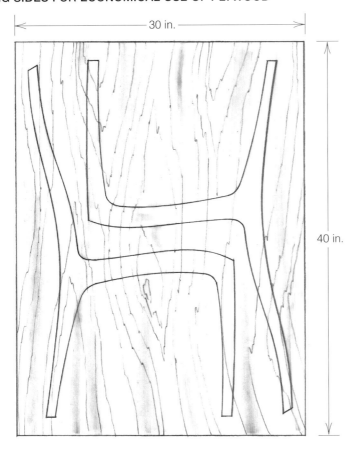

← 30 in. →

40 in.

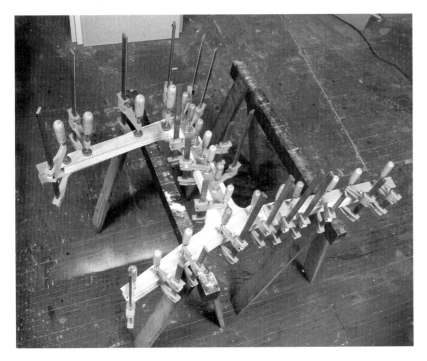

It takes a lot of clamps to glue up the two plywood layers for a chair side. Make sure you have them at hand before you start the process. Notice that I've protected the chair sides with pads made out of ¼-in. plywood strips.

I've chosen Baltic Birch, Apple Ply, or a similar plywood because of their even, void-free plies and attractive edge; but splintering of the face veneers can be a problem on these.

Enlarge and cut out the pattern (refer again to the drawing on p. 58), and drill 3/32-in. holes to locate the centers of the dowel holes. Then trace the pattern onto the plywood. To make it easier to glue the double thicknesses together, precut the four sides for the two double-thickness chair sides. You may need to use a jigsaw for some of the cutting, especially to start, because this shape will be somewhere between awkward and impossible to cut on a bandsaw depending on the throat depth of the saw. Plan out your cuts carefully. Cut well to the outside of the lines, so splintering isn't a problem. Glue the precut parts together with as many clamps as you can muster (see the photo on p. 61). Then cut to the line, sand the edges smooth, and rout the edges with a 3/8-in. roundover bit.

If you've got access to a vacuum press, this is a perfect time to use it. It will save you precutting the parts. Just glue up a large enough piece (30 in. by 40 in.) of double-thickness plywood, and then cut and sand the chair sides to shape. (See the drawing on p. 61 for an economical way to nest the sides on the plywood.)

Drilling the holes
Once the sides are shaped, the process of drilling and assembling the chair is the same whether the sides are solid or plywood. Cut the dowels to 17 7/8 in., so you can get two out of each 36-in. dowel length. But before you start drilling the chair sides, there is some more work that needs to be done.

The first step is to figure out what size hole to drill. Drill a test hole in a block of the same wood you are using for the actual chair, and try a few of the dowels in it. They should fit tightly: too tight to insert more than 1/4 in. or so. If you need to adjust the hole size to get this tight fit, try a different style of drill bit (for example, a brad point, spade bit, or forstner, if you're using a twist drill), or try a different size (such as a metric, letter, or number-size drill bit). Drill all of the holes to this size on the drill press. Set the depth to 7/8 in. for the seat holes. If you have tapered the upper part of the rear legs, the holes will get progressively shallower toward the top of the back.

Shrinking the dowels
Here's a trick I use to make assembly easier. I shrink the ends of the dowels so they slip into the holes without my having to resort to excessive force. Follow the procedure in the sidebar on the facing page, then check the fit again in one of the holes in the chair sides. The dowels should fit much more easily. If you need a little more shrinking, repeat the same process. Then turn the dowels over, and shrink the other side. Once both ends of the dowels have been dried, move on to the assembly. The dowels do pick up moisture from the air. They can be noticeably tighter within 12 hours on a humid day.

Assembling the chair
Start by getting everything ready for the assembly. You will need a slow-setting glue (white glue or a slow-setting epoxy works well), a length of 3/8-in. dowel or a small brush to spread the glue in the holes, four or five (or more) 2-ft. clamps with clamp pads, and a nonmarring mallet—all within convenient reach of an uncluttered work surface. A fine-tooth handsaw may be neces-

DOWELS AND HOLES — PART 2

As mentioned earlier, dowel sizes are variable. When building the real dowel chairs, there is an additional factor involved: Not only do the dowels have to fit in the holes, but they also need to fit tightly. A good fit holds the chair solidly together and keeps it from wobbling. But a fit tight enough for this is usually too tight for reasonable assembly. The solution is to temporarily shrink the ends of the dowels by drying them out thoroughly. This process can shrink the dowels by as much as $\frac{1}{100}$ in. (It will also cause the dowels to become slightly oval in shape, but this shouldn't be a problem.) When the dowels are glued into place, they will absorb moisture from the surrounding wood, the air, and the glue (if it is water-based) and expand to a tighter fit. This is really the only way to make this chair successfully.

Here's how to do it. Fill an old 5-lb. coffee can or metal bucket halfway with sand, and set this on a hot plate (see the photo at right). It takes about 30 minutes at medium heat to get the sand to the right temperature. Mix the sand around a few times before you put the dowels in because the temperature can vary by more than 100°F from the bottom to the top of the sand. The sand should be about 170° to 180°F when measured with a meat thermometer inserted about 2 in. deep into the sand. Stick the dowels in to this same depth. Avoid resting any against the edge of the can, or they may scorch. Then turn off the heat and unplug the hot plate. Check a few of the dowels after 5 minutes to be sure they are not scorching in the sand or checking (cracking or splitting) on the ends from drying too rapidly. If they are, remove them all for 10 or 15 minutes to allow the sand to cool down a little. Then let the dowels sit in the sand for an hour or two.

The dowel-shrinking apparatus is working its magic. A meat thermometer (inside the can) is used for checking the temperature of the sand.

sary, too. Make sure that the temperature in the room is at least 60°F, or you risk the glue turning chalky instead of sticking. Spread the glue into all of the holes on one side of the chair. Try to put just enough glue in the holes to coat the walls and no more. A lot of squeeze-out is not fun to deal with on this chair. (If glue does squeeze out, a sharp knife with a bevel on only one side will help you get in between the dowels. Wait until the glue is rubbery hard before trying to remove it.) Insert all of the dowels into the glued side. Tap each dowel down with the mallet to make sure it is seated all the way before proceeding to the next one. (Listen for the change in sound when the dowel is seated all the way.)

Before moving on to the other side frame, check to see if any of the dowels are sticking up higher than

Guide one dowel at a time into its hole as you work across the seat of the chair. Tighten the second clamp just a bit before moving on to the next hole.

want to bang this chair together because the fit will be tighter than the test chair, the wood is less compressible, and you will probably mar the surface somewhat.

Once you have two or three dowels in place, put a clamp (with clamp pads) across the front of the chair. Don't tighten it much just yet; for now, it's there mostly to keep these first dowels from popping out when you try to get the rest in place. Put another clamp at the point where the seat turns up and becomes the back. Then carefully fit the next dowel into its hole, tighten the second clamp very slightly, and move on to the next one the same way (see the photo at left). Keep checking a few dowels ahead because the dowels don't always cooperate as fully as you wish they would. With the dowels for the seat in place, place a clamp across the top of the back, and proceed up the back just as you did across the seat (see the photo on the facing page).

Once the dowels are all in place, you will need to add more clamps so you can press the dowels all the way in. Tighten slowly and evenly so you don't distort the sides of the chair. Check the width of the chair all along the glue-up to verify that the dowels are all seated. If a dowel bends under the clamp pressure (the glue may have started to set), push in on the bulge, and the dowel will usually seat a little farther. Once you're sure that the chair is completely together, you should be able to take the clamps off.

Finishing the chair
This chair may be easy to build, but finishing all of those dowels is a bit of a chore. Oil and wax is still a good way to go (see the appendix on

the rest. If you can't tap the problem dowels down, you'll have to cut them off at the same height as the rest with a handsaw before proceeding. Now, spread the glue in the holes on the opposite side. Invert the side with the dowels in it, and lift it into place over the side you just glued. Start at the front of the seat, and angle the chair so you can get the first dowel into the appropriate hole. Tap this down gently, then position the next dowel. You don't

Inserting dowels in the back of the chair is the same as when you inserted dowels across the seat.

p. 195 for a description of my preferred method). If you are diligent about wiping off extra oil, especially around and in between the dowels, you'll avoid the biggest problems.

Installing glides

Installing glides is usually the last step. Sometimes it makes sense to do this earlier, however. If you'll be moving the chair around a lot or sending it out for finishing or upholstery (as with the other chairs in this book), it's a very good idea to protect the leg bottoms before anything happens to them.

Pad a workbench with a blanket, some clean rags, or something comparable. Invert the chair, and rest the seat on the padding. Mark out the centers of the leg bottoms, and tack the glides in carefully. On this chair, I used the plastic type with an embedded nail. I always get a little tense about this—for some reason, I always expect the leg to split apart when I hammer in the glides. But this is just the fear of having all my work undone by the last step, and nothing like that has ever happened. This is *not* something to worry about. But if you're still worried, predrill the legs using a drill bit a little smaller than the nail on the glide.

Have a seat! You should have a very comfortable chair and a much better understanding of what goes into making a chair feel that way.

4

RIGHT-ANGLE CHAIR

From our study of comfort and curves in Chapter 3, we move to a study of what we can do with straight lines and right angles. We don't exactly abandon comfort, but the goal of this chapter is very different from that of Chapter 3: to acquaint you with the basic frame chair and to introduce mortise-and-tenon joinery.

The sheer quantity of joinery on a chair like this is enough to intimidate some people. If that describes your feelings when considering this project, I should mention that one of the lessons to be learned in chairmaking is how chair joinery can be systematized. There are fewer setups required than you might imagine, and cutting the joints is actually rather quick. I enjoy the joinery tremendously; that is what transforms the project from a pile of sticks into a chair. I usually find that the slowest part of the job is the smoothing/ sanding/finishing phase.

The basic frame chair is the foundation on which thousands of chair designs are built. At its simplest, the frame chair has two front legs and two taller rear legs, which allow for some type of back support, joined by four rails. Straight lines and right angles are a real design challenge: There just aren't that many ways to make a comfortable chair within these constraints. So, as a rule, the back must be angled back for acceptable comfort. On this chair, the only place that there is anything other than a straight line is on the rear legs, which angle back from above the seat. Vertical slats are usually more comfortable than horizontal ones, especially on a chair without curves. To avoid angled tenons at the bottoms of these slats, the slats run between horizontal rails. We wind up with more joints to cut, but the joints are simpler. The vertical slats also help with an entirely different problem inherent in chairs with right angles and straight lines: Due to a quirk of perception, the back of a chair like this usually looks wider than the front. Most chairs that appear to have well-proportioned rectangular seats actually narrow slightly toward the back. The narrower back-slat structure helps just a little with this.

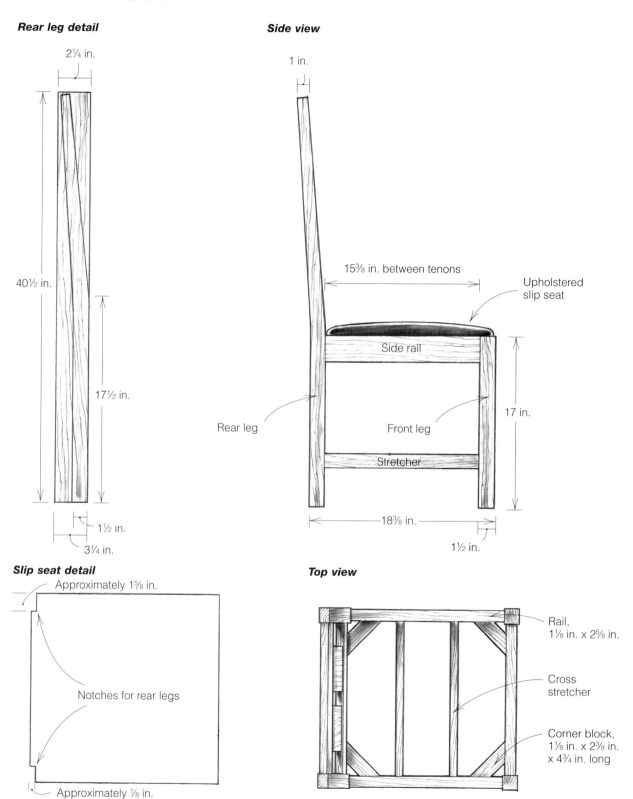

Rear leg detail

2¼ in.

40½ in.

17½ in.

1½ in.

3¼ in.

Side view

1 in.

15⅜ in. between tenons

Upholstered
slip seat

Side rail

Rear leg

Front leg

17 in.

Stretcher

18⅜ in.

1½ in.

Slip seat detail

Approximately 1⅝ in.

Notches for rear legs

Approximately ⅛ in.

Top view

Rail,
1⅛ in. x 2⅝ in.

Cross
stretcher

Corner block,
1⅛ in. x 2⅜ in.
x 4¾ in. long

Front view

Side view detail of back slat joinery

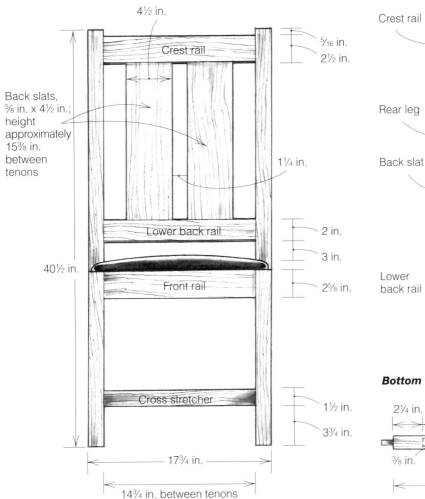

4½ in.

Crest rail

Back slats,
⅝ in. x 4½ in.;
height
approximately
15⅜ in.
between
tenons

5/16 in.
2½ in.

1¼ in.

Lower back rail

2 in.
3 in.

40½ in.

Front rail

2⅝ in.

Cross stretcher

1½ in.
3¾ in.

17¾ in.

14¾ in. between tenons

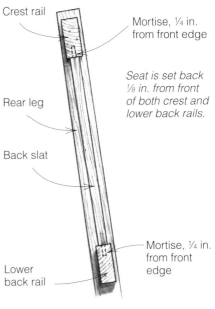

Crest rail

Mortise, ¼ in.
from front edge

*Seat is set back
⅛ in. from front
of both crest and
lower back rails.*

Rear leg

Back slat

Lower
back rail

Mortise, ¼ in.
from front
edge

Bottom view detail of crest rail mortise

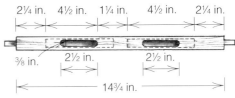

2¼ in. 4½ in. 1¼ in. 4½ in. 2¼ in.

⅜ in. 2½ in. 2½ in.

14¾ in.

Stretcher detail

Side stretcher,
13/16 in. x 1½ in.

Cross stretcher,
13/16 in. x 1½ in.

4½ in.

Twin tenon detail

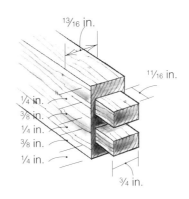

13/16 in.

11/16 in.

¼ in.
⅜ in.
¼ in.
⅜ in.
¼ in.

¾ in.

Use the end of a board to mark the rip fence where the saw kerf begins for a stopped cut. The board is at the point just before the blade starts to cut. Unplug the saw before doing this.

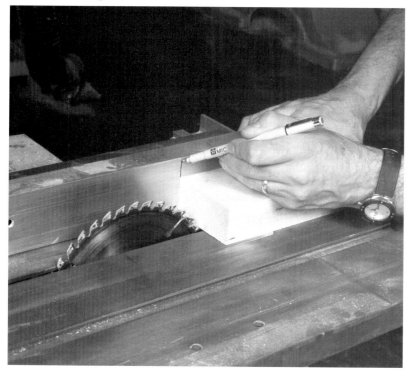

PREPARING THE CHAIR PARTS

Start by getting together the necessary wood for the project and looking it over carefully (see the drawing on pp. 68-69 for dimensions on all parts). The back slats of this chair are a focal point and should have the most interesting wood. It could even be a different wood. For my chair, I found a piece of 8/4 bird's-eye maple to go with the plain maple of the rest of the chair. I resawed the bird's-eye on the bandsaw so I would have book-matched slats. If you do resaw, let the wood rest for a few days to allow for stresses and moisture imbalances in the wood to settle. Then plane the two halves to ⅝ in. thick. Keep in mind that book-matched slats are nice—they are a good way to heighten the visual interest of whatever wood you use—but they aren't necessary as long as you find well-matched pieces. If you're making a set of chairs, look for enough wood to have the backs all match. The rest of the chair should have wood of uniform grain and color, as much as possible.

Cutting and shaping the legs, rails, and stretchers

For the front legs, plane 8/4 stock down to 1½ in. thick, joint one edge straight and square, and rip off a piece a little over 1½ in. wide.

Check the cut edge on the remaining stock to be sure it is straight and square, joint if necessary, and rip another leg. Repeat until you have the front legs you need. Then rip the rear legs to 3¼ in. wide. Plane all of the front legs to 1½ in. square. Be sure to reference off the square edge when planing. Throughout your work, you should constantly pay attention to keeping stock square. It pays off every step of the way. It also becomes more automatic over time.

Next, cut the rear legs to shape. Mark out the shape of the back on the leg blanks (see the back leg detail in the drawing on pp. 68-69). Start with cutting the lower leg. Set the rip fence on the tablesaw to a little over 1½ in., and make a mark on the fence to indicate where the saw kerf begins (see the photo at left). Orient the leg with the front against the fence and the bottom facing forward (toward the blade), then make a mark to indicate where the cut should stop—16½ in. up from the bottom. Now cut until the mark on the leg is lined up with the mark on the fence (see the photo on the facing page). Then while holding everything firmly in place, shut off the saw. *Don't move* until the saw blade has stopped. If this stopped cut makes you uneasy or if you can't access the switch comfortably while holding the work in place, just make the cut on the bandsaw, and smooth with hand planes and so on.

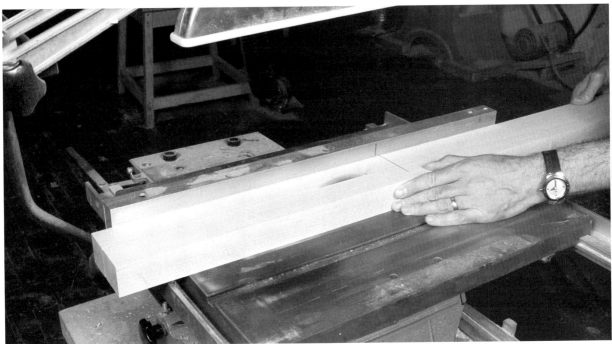

The rest of the cuts are made on the bandsaw anyway.

When cutting the angled front of the upper leg, stay about ⅛ in. to the outside of the line to allow room for smoothing the bandsawn edge without ending up planing away wood where the side rail will join the leg. On the other lines, keep to the outside, but try to stay close. Then carefully joint or hand-plane the bandsawn front edge of the leg. The transition area between the upper and lower sections on the front of the leg should be rounded over slightly—just enough to eliminate a hard edge. You can plane most of the back edge with a regular smooth plane, especially if it is angled across the leg. The transition between the upper and lower sections on the back can be scraped and sanded, but I use a compass plane. The back could also be belt-sanded or flush-trimmed (see the sidebar on p. 38). Remember to stay away from the ends.

Note that you can use the waste stock from the rear legs for making the stretchers or even for the front legs, if you choose.

The front, back, lower back, and side rails are all cut from 6/4 stock, milled to 1⅛ in., or you can purchase surfaced 5/4 wood, which will be 1¹/₁₆ in. thick. This is not a critical dimension, and I've used anything from 1 in. to 1½ in. for rails, depending on what I have around at the time. The crest rail is ⅞ in. thick and can be milled or resawn to this thickness. Stretchers are ¹³/₁₆ in. thick; because they are 1½ in. wide, they can be ripped from leftover leg stock. Leave the stretchers long for now. Cut the rails to width, but leave them long for now also.

Laying out the leg mortises
When laying out the joinery locations on the chair stock, keep in mind how you're going to cut the joinery. If you are hand-chopping

When making the stopped cut for the bottom portion of the rear legs, watch the marks on both the rip fence and the workpiece. The visible part of the saw blade is not close to the line, but the line is almost to the mark on the fence, which indicates that the blade is almost to the line on the bottom of the board.

TENONS FOR THIS CHAIR

All of these tenons are ⅜ in. thick and ⅞ in. long.

Tenons centered on rail

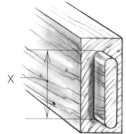

Side stretchers X = 1 in.
Lower back rail X = 1½ in.
Back slats X = 2½ in.

Tenons offset down

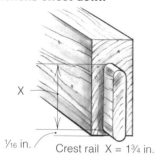

¹⁄₁₆ in.   Crest rail X = 1¾ in.

Tenons offset to the outside

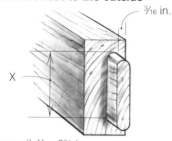

³⁄₁₆ in.

Rear rail X = 2⅜ in.
Back of side rails X = 2⅜ in.

Tenons offset down and to the outside

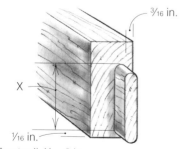

³⁄₁₆ in.

¹⁄₁₆ in.

Front rail X = 2 in.
Front of side rails X = 2 in.

"LEFT" AND "RIGHT" MORTISES

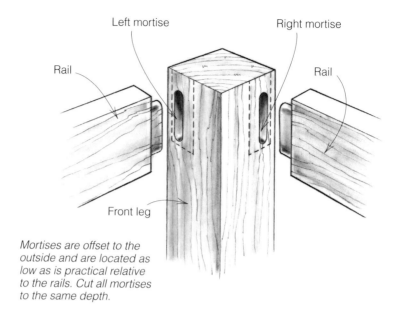

Left mortise

Right mortise

Rail

Rail

Front leg

Mortises are offset to the outside and are located as low as is practical relative to the rails. Cut all mortises to the same depth.

mortises, you need every line carefully scribed. But it is not necessary to lay out all of the lines for every joint if you'll be relying on power tools and jigs to do the locating and sizing for you. For example, all of the rail mortises in the legs can be cut with the same basic setup. Only one leg should be marked out for the distance of the mortise from the edge, and it's probably best if that one is marked on an extra board, so you can test your setup before working on the actual stock. With this in mind, only the tops and bottoms of the leg-to-rail mortises need to be marked. And if you are using a jig that has stops to limit the router travel at the tops and bottoms of mortises, then only two mortises—one "left" side and one "right" side—need to be marked out exactly. "Left" and "right" are not descriptive of where on the *chair* the mortise is located, but rather where on each *leg*. This is a convenient way to describe the asymmetry of the joints on

each leg (see the drawing above). It is still very important that you make some indication of exactly what needs to be cut where, so that you don't use a jig that has been carefully set up to cut a joint in the wrong side or on the wrong end of a leg. These marks can be as quick and simple as pencil lines.

On this chair, all of the mortises for the seat rail joints are offset to the outside to allow for longer tenons on the rails. On the front legs, they are located on the lower part of where the rails go to keep them as far as possible from the tops of the front legs (see the dotted lines on the drawing above for this orientation). Since this is not a factor on the rear legs, these mortises can extend up a little higher, and the tenons can be almost the full width of the rails.

If you have a scrap of leg stock long enough to safely cut test joints in, mark out a test mortise ¼ in. from one edge (the mortise length doesn't matter). If you don't have any extra leg stock, fully mark out an actual mortise on one of the legs. Then mark out the tops and bottoms of all of the mortises accurately, and indicate left-side or right-side locations with a pencil mark.

Locate the rest of the mortises in a similar way. The crest and lower back rail mortises both reference off the front edge of the rear leg. The crest rail is basically centered on the leg; center the top of the rail and don't worry about the leg taper. The lower back rail is the same distance back from the front edge of the leg. Center the stretcher mortises on the legs. (Wait until the length of the slats has been determined to lay out and cut mortises in the crest and lower back rails.)

Cutting the leg mortises

I used the mortising block described in the sidebar on p. 43 with a plunge router and fence to cut all of the mortises on this chair. Whatever method you choose, the basics will be similar.

Set the depth of cut first because this is easier before other parameters have been set. Use the depth stop on the router for this. The side-to-side location of the mortise is next. With the mortising block, this is controlled by the router fence. If you marked out a scrap, make a test cut in this piece, then measure to be sure the location is correct. If you have to work with an actual leg, make a very shallow test cut—barely making a mark on the leg—then measure and correct if necessary. The length and the top and bottom locations can be controlled two different ways. You can rely on your eyes and rout to the lines. Or you can clamp or screw stops to the mortising block to make things a little more definite. If you do this, you'll also need to have a way to consistently locate the workpiece in the jig. An adjustable stop block—either screwed or clamped in place—to register the top or bottom of the workpiece is ideal.

Whatever refinements you make, be sure to hold the plunge router and fence tight against the block *at all times*. Never start or stop the router while it is in contact with the workpiece; always start at and return to what I call "tray-table position"—fully upright and locked. When cutting, take very light passes. Try not to plunge down more than $1/16$ in. at a time, even less in harder woods. If the router sounds like it's straining, you're plunging too deeply. This is important for consistent fit as the router bit may deflect and cut a larger hole when overworked. Cutting mortises with a plunge router takes a little practice. Try some mortises in scrap if you haven't done much of this before.

Lay the chair parts out in a logical fashion. I usually arrange the parts in a "home position," where their position on the actual chair is obvious (at least to me). This helps me to keep track of what I'm working on at all times (see the drawing on p. 74). Now proceed to mortise in a systematic way. This is especially important when making more than one chair, but it cuts down the work of even one. Make all of the left-side cuts, then change setups if necessary, and cut the right sides. Always return the parts to their home position. Then switch to the cuts that are centered. Finally, do any remaining mortises that require individual setups.

Cutting rails and stretchers to size

The rails and stretchers are still over-sized. To come up with an exact length for each part, first check the mortise depths. I like to cut tenons about $\frac{1}{32}$ in. (or less) shorter than the depth of the mortises to leave room for any excess glue and to ensure that the tenon won't bottom out before the shoulder is tight. Once you know the necessary tenon size, add the desired length of the rail or stretcher between tenons to come up with the exact length for each rail or stretcher. On this chair, all of the mortises are the same depth. So be sure to cut all of the parts that will have the same between-tenon length (rails and side stretchers) to the same overall length. This way, the same setup can be used to cut the tenons, and the result should be equal lengths between the tenons. Leave the cross stretchers oversized until later.

This is a good time to lay out and cut the mortises for the back slats in the crest and lower back rails. Locate the mortises $\frac{1}{4}$ in. from the front face of both rails, and center them on the slat locations (see the detail of back slat joinery on p. 69).

Laying out the tenons

The principles we discussed for mortise layout also apply to tenons. If a jig or machine will take care of the location and/or size, you should only lay out what you need to help set up the jig. All other similar joints can be simply marked for identification and orientation. It is even more important than when cutting the mortises that you lay out and cut a joint on an identically dimensioned scrap (use cutoffs that are long enough to work on safely) to test the fit and alignment before you cut the real tenons.

Use a marking gauge set to the desired tenon length to scribe the

---

MAINTAINING ORDER WHILE MORTISING

Home position

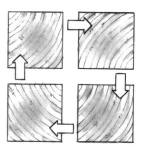

First cut the mortises on these faces (all of the left mortises).

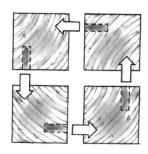

Then cut all of the right mortises (change the setup if necessary).

shoulder line of a test tenon. If you have a mortise-and-marking gauge—the kind with two points or knives on one side that can be set a fixed distance apart, and one point or knife on the other—you can use this for the actual tenon layout. Since we are using jigs where the setup can be tested and the cuts can be repeated accurately, marking so precisely is not essential. In addition, the rails are set in from the legs between $\frac{1}{16}$ in. and $\frac{3}{32}$ inch. This is a significant factor in making the chair easier to build. It gives a little leeway in the tenon locations, enough to allow for marking the tenons directly from the mortises by hand.

To mark out a tenon by hand, set the leg down on a work surface, mortise facing up. Lay the rail or a test piece on the leg on edge—oriented with the good face out—so the end rests in the middle of the mortise. Now adjust the rail so it is set in from the outside of the leg the desired amount (see above). Mark the tenon location from the mortise on the top of the rail with a pencil or a knife (see the top photo at right). Extend these lines across the top with a square, or use your fingers and a pencil as a sort of marking gauge (as shown). Then lay the rail down on its face and rotate it 90 degrees so the top edge is flush with the top of the leg. (On a rear leg, measure up from the bottom to be sure the rail is at the proper height.) Then mark the top and bottom of the tenon the same way you marked the sides, and extend these lines across the top as well (see the bottom photo at right). Transfer the marks you will need to cut the rest of the tenons from one to another by holding the rails together and marking with a pencil and a square.

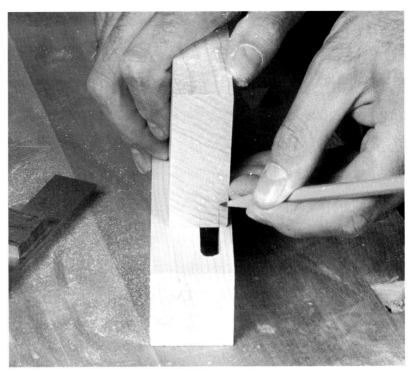

I like to mark out tenons by hand. When cutting tenons by machine, this is a good approach; it's easy, fast, and accurate enough for most situations. Don't forego cutting a test tenon, though. Notice that the rail is set in from the edge of the leg.

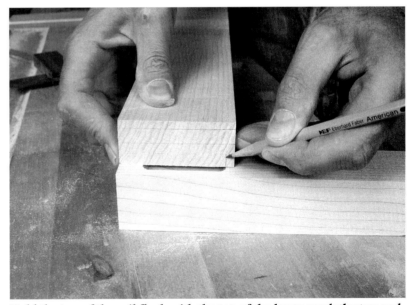

Hold the top of the rail flush with the top of the leg to mark the top and bottom of the tenon. It helps to support the other end of the rail on another leg.

Cutting the tenons

I used the tenoning jig described in the sidebar on p. 46 and a plunge router to cut most of the tenons for this chair. The tablesaw also works quite well because there are no angled tenons. If you're using the tenoning jig, clamp it in your workbench vise. Then clamp the marked-out test piece into place snug to the fence and up against the bottom of the template. Set the tenon length by adjusting the plunge router's depth stop. The point of the router bit should just touch the scribed shoulder line. Then remove the router, and adjust the position of the tenoning template so that it is just centered on the marked lines on the top of the work-piece. Screw or clamp the template into place, then check to be sure it is still in the proper place.

Now cut a test tenon. For best results, cut with many light passes. The proper way to cut a tenon is to start the router with the bit all the way up, then plunge down to the preset depth. The first pass should be a very light climb cut—a cut made with the router traveling in the same direction that the bit would propel it if it were a wheel (see the drawing below). This lessens the chance of tearout. In this situation, a climb cut is relatively easy to control and is very useful. Then take several passes in the corect direction to complete one side of the tenon. When one

CLIMB CUTTING WITH A TENONING JIG

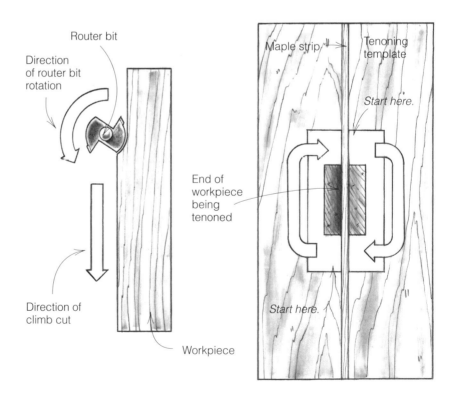

To prevent tearout, initial cut should be a climb cut. Successive cuts should be made in the correct direction to complete one side of the tenon.

side of the tenon is complete, raise the router up, shut down, and wait for the router to come to a complete stop. Then repeat the procedure for the other side of the tenon.

The tenon won't fit into the mortise yet because the top and bottom shoulders haven't been created. Transfer the lines around from the end of the tenon to the cheek, then rough-cut the waste on the bandsaw or tablesaw, clean up the shoulders with a sharp chisel, and round over the ends of the tenons (see p. 32 for more on this).

Now test the tenon. If it's too loose, try putting some masking tape on the bearing surfaces of the tenon template. Or try a router bit that has been sharpened and therefore has a smaller diameter; it will remove less wood. If the tenon is too tight, the options are fewer for correcting the fit. Unless you cut the tenons with a router bit that has been sharpened at least once and have an unsharpened

bit handy, you're not likely to find a bit with a larger diameter. It may be necessary to hand-fit the tenon (which is not a big problem).

But before you do that, there are two other options—one simple and one not so simple—to consider. Check to see if the router bit is concentric with the guide bushing. If it is not, as is often the case with plunge routers in particular, you may be able to change the width of the tenon by referencing a different point of the router base against the tenoning jig. This works because at different places the guide bushing is closer to or farther away from the router bit. In this situation, you want the guide bushing closer to the bit. You need to be consistent in how you hold the router. A reference mark taped onto the router base can help you keep the router rotated to the proper angle. If this trick doesn't help, you might just want to remake the tenon template with a slightly narrower guide bar. All of the effort that

HOW TO ACHIEVE JOINTS THAT FIT WELL

What is a good fit? I define a good fit as one where you can push the joint together by hand with some force. You shouldn't need clamps or a hammer. But the joint shouldn't be so loose that it will fall apart by itself.

There are a few factors that have a clear effect on the way joints will fit. One is the wood. Different woods compress more or less easily. A tight joint in pine may fit together well. A joint sized exactly the same in hard maple may not go together at all without refitting. The harder the wood, the closer the tolerance required for a good fit.

The jig is another obvious factor. If it isn't sized properly, the fit will suffer. But there may be problems even with a well-sized jig. Sawdust can build up on the template and effectively change the template size. As mentioned above, the guide bushing may not be concentric with the bit. And the template can flex a little. To minimize this,

you should always cut joints with a light touch. Each pass should remove just what the router can handle without any strain. Be sure the final pass is made with good contact between the guide bushing and template, but don't force it. Forcing or overworking the router introduces other inaccuracies. When the router is overworked, the router bit is likely to "whip": The end of the router bit starts to travel in a slightly larger circle, cutting a larger path than the size of the bit.

You are a factor, too. The amount of pressure you apply and how fast you cut will affect how the bit cuts. The rotational angle of the router may affect the distance between the template and the actual cut. You control these things. The more sensitive you are to the variables, the more consistent your joints will be. Of course, on some days, it seems like the alignment of the planets affects the fit. Experience suggests that this is not really true. It is usually the tides that are causing the trouble!

CUTTING TWIN MORTISE-AND-TENON JOINTS

Twin mortise-and-tenon joints are good to use where a rail is oriented across the board it is to join. The mortises for these parallel tenons are easy to cut with a ⅜-in. bit in a plunge router and the mortising block. Mark out the mortises, and make them ¾ in. long. You can either reference off of both sides of the stretcher to make the cuts, or reset the router fence. With the latter, cut one of the mortises on each of the parts before shifting the fence, then finish the joint. This is a situation where chiseling the ends of the mortises square makes a difference. The glue surface is increased significantly on such a short joint.

Since the router tenoning jig doesn't work for this kind of tenon, I cut the twin tenons on the tablesaw and bandsaw. Start by cutting the shoulders on the 1½-in.-wide sides of the stretchers on the tablesaw. Lower the blade until it is just ¹⁄₃₂ in. above the table surface. Then, using the miter gauge and the rip fence as a stop to control the tenon length, cut the shoulders. Take multiple passes to clear away the wood. Now mark the actual tenon locations on the freshly cut cheeks (see the top photo at right). Cut the shoulders on the other two faces of the stretchers: Either raise the blade to cut all the way up to the marked lines, or just cut at the same setting to make a clean shoulder. Extend the marks for the two inside faces of the tenons all the way up the cheek on the side of the rail, and cut away the waste between the tenons. You can use the bandsaw (see the bottom photo at right) to cut the tenon cheeks, then "nibble" away at the waste inside, or you can use the tablesaw with a tenoning jig to help hold the stretcher upright. Use a chisel to clean up the work, especially in the space between the tenons.

Mark the locations for the cheeks of the twin tenons on the newly cut surface.

Finish up the twin tenons on the bandsaw. Cut the inside cheeks, then nibble away at the waste in between. Be careful not to cut into the shoulder. You can clean out any excess wood with a chisel.

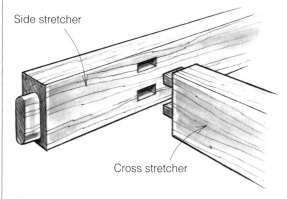

Side stretcher

Cross stretcher

The tenons are small, but they have good long-grain surfaces and make a strong glue joint.

goes into making a good fit will be repaid, especially on a chair like this where all of the tenons are the same thickness.

Once the test tenon fits well, it's time to cut the real things. As with the mortises, lay the chair parts out in an organized manner. Again, this is especially important when making multiple chairs, but it helps to have all of the parts to be cut with one set-up together and marked appropriately. Check that each chair part is aligned correctly in the jig, with no sawdust interfering, then cut carefully. When finished with the first setup, test out the alignment of the next, and cut those joints.

Unfortunately, the tenons are not quite done. Trim the ends to size, and round over the ends with a rasp (or square the ends of the mortises with a chisel) as you did on the test tenon. Clean up the corners of the shoulders, if necessary, with a chisel. Don't fuss too much over a perfect half-round tenon or a squared mortise. Just get the tenon to fit the mortise. For those tenons that meet in intersecting mortises, miter the tenon ends just enough to prevent interference between meeting tenons. (Be sure to miter the *inside* corner.) This is not a precision operation either. Cut by eye on the bandsaw, or take a few swipes with a hand plane.

Fitting the joints

This is where the chair starts to look like something. Joint by joint, go around the chair and make sure that the tenons fit. Trim down any that are too tight with a shoulder plane or a rasp (see p. 34), and patch and refit any that are too loose. As you go, mark both sides of each joint with a unique letter, number, or whatever helps to eliminate confusion later. Then dry-assemble the not-quite-complete chair frame for a psychological boost.

While the chair is together, measure the distance between the crest rail and the lower back rail to determine the length of the back slats between tenons. Measure the distance between the stretchers, too; you may need to clamp the rails tightly together to get an exact measurement. Then disassemble the chair. Be very careful when pulling (or tapping) the seat frame apart. If one side comes off first and you're still pulling hard, you can easily crack the joint on the leg that is still together.

Making the back slats

Calculate the overall length of the back slats by adding the tenon lengths (equal to the mortise depths less $1/32$ in.) to the measured between-tenon length. Then lay out the tenons centered on the ends of the slats. Cut, trim, round over the sides (I called them the top and bottom on all of the horizontal tenons, but these are vertical), and test the fit. When all four tenons fit well, dry-assemble the slats with the crest and lower back rails, and clamp together. Take the dry-assembled back and check to see if the rail tenons fit in the rail mortises in the legs. If the slat length is a little off, trim down the crest-rail tenons so everything fits together.

Making the stretchers

For this chair, I chose stretchers that connect the front and rear legs, joined by a pair of cross stretchers that run from side to side. This structure of the stretchers relates well to the structure of back. For those of us who worry about structural details, this arrangement of stretchers is more complicated than it might at first seem. The problem is in the joints between the side stretchers and the cross stretchers. The usual temptation—for those who aren't inclined to just screw and plug—is to use mortise-and-tenon joints. But a typical mortise and tenon doesn't work well in this situation. There is no real long-grain-to-long-grain glue surface.

There are two completely correct—and admittedly obsessive—solutions. (Of course, there is also the option of being less than completely correct.) The first of the two correct solutions is to cut *twin* mortise-and-tenon joints (see the sidebar on p. 78 for how to cut twin mortise-and-tenon joints). This joint is very good in a variety of situations where a rail is oriented across the board it is to join, although it is not widely used. The mortises run with the grain, while the tenons run across the *width* of the stretcher. A single tenon this short would not normally provide enough glue surface. Two parallel tenons will increase the glue surface to an acceptable level.

A sliding dovetail joint is the other possibility. This still has minimal long-grain-to-long-grain glue surface, but it has very good mechanical strength. This should be cut so that it is only visible from the bottom of the chair because none of the other joinery on the chair shows.

Smoothing the parts
After the joints are cut, all of the surfaces must be smoothed. This is an easy chair to smooth because, except for the rear legs, it is entirely straight lines. Be very careful not to round over or angle any of the areas around the mortises. As discussed in Chapter 2, my preference is to try a hand plane first because it leaves the best surface and is also the fastest. If that doesn't work, I move on to scraping and sanding. Ease all of the

edges either by planing, by routing a slight chamfer, or by breaking the edges with a little sandpaper. Be sure to chamfer all four edges on the bottoms of the legs. This should be a little bigger chamfer than on the rest of the chair (about $\frac{1}{16}$ in.) because it helps protect the legs.

ASSEMBLING THE CHAIR
Collect all of the parts, clamps, clamp pads and/or cauls, glue, and glue spreader (I use a thin piece of wood) in a convenient place for the glue-up. You'll also need some small pieces of wood to temporarily fill mortises to keep them from being crushed by the clamp pressure when assembling sections of the chair. Tenons cut for test fitting are perfect for this, but any $\frac{3}{8}$-in.-thick stock will do. (Check the fit in the mortises.)

Assemble the chair in stages to avoid the panic of trying to glue and clamp everything together at once. The back slats and rails go together first. Spread the glue in the slat mortises on the crest and lower back rails, then spread a very thin film on the slat tenons. Wiping a little on and then wiping it off with your fingers would leave the proper amount, but then your fingers would have glue on them. Once that happens, glue smudges get everywhere. So think of that as the ideal, but wipe the glue off with the glue spreader instead. Put the back slats and rails together, and clamp using clamp pads or cauls to protect the rails.

The stretcher assembly is next. Spread glue in the mortises or in the sliding dovetails, then insert the cross stretchers, and clamp. If you're using dovetails and have a tight fit, you shouldn't need to leave the

When clamping the front leg assembly, insert fillers into the mortises to avoid crushing the mortises.

clamps on. With a less-than-perfect fit, you should leave the clamps across the joints, and tap in a thin wedge or two to tighten up the joint.

Next, move on to the front legs and front rail. Spread glue in the front rail mortises and lightly on the tenons, then put the front assembly together. Insert the ³⁄₈-in.-thick mortise-filler stock partway into the side rail mortises, and clamp (see the photo above). Leave this assembly lying down with the mortises facing up so that excess glue doesn't run into the joints.

When the glue is dry, take the stretcher assembly out of clamps, and check the joints to see if they are flush. If they need work, now is the time to do it—a random-orbit sander works well.

When the back assembly comes out of the clamps, you can put the complete back together. Spread glue in the appropriate rear leg mortises— and not in the mortises for the side rails or the side stretchers—and also lightly on all of the back rail tenons. Check the orientation of all of the parts one last time, then insert the rails into one of the legs. Pick up the partially assembled back, turn it over, and work on getting the tenons into the mortises in the other rear leg. Once all are started in the proper places, stick the mortise fillers partway into the side rail mortises, and start clamping the back together. You will need two or three clamps to get all of the rails tight. Leave this assembly with the side-rail mortises facing up. When the front and back are dry, unclamp them, and move on to the final glue-up. Check the mortises in the legs for any glue that may have come through, and clean it out with a chisel if necessary. Spread glue, insert the rails and stretchers, and apply the clamps. Tighten the clamps slowly and evenly.

FINISHING TOUCHES

There's a great deal of satisfaction in seeing your chair together. It may seem like it's done but there are a few tasks yet to do. While you're working on the finish, you will probably want to move on to working on the corner blocks, the seat blank, and the upholstery, so everything can come together dramatically and satisfyingly when you're done.

Finshing

Finish the chair however you choose. I outlined my usual oil-and-wax finish in the appendix (see p. 195). This leaves a very smooth surface that holds up well.

Adding corner blocks

Corner blocks are an essential part of a joined chair. Not only do they reinforce the chair's critical joints, but they also provide a good place to attach the seat. The corner blocks for this chair are cut from $1\frac{1}{8}$-in. by $2\frac{3}{8}$-in. stock and are roughly $4\frac{3}{4}$ in. long with 45-degree angles on both ends. They each have four screw holes. Cut them on the tablesaw with the blade tilted to 45 degrees. Then drill the holes for the screws on the drill press. To do this, clamp a fence with a simple stop to the drill press table. Then clamp or hold the corner block bevel down, and drill with a bit and countersink. You'll get two of the holes on each corner block with the same setup, then you'll have to move the stop to cut the other two.

Sand off any fuzz, then screw the blocks into place, centered top to bottom on the rails.

Preparing the seat blank

The seat blank is the part that will be upholstered, then attached to the chair. Once upholstered, it is also called a slip seat, although technically a slip seat is (or at least it was) a seat that "slips" into place in a rabbet in the rails. The upholstered piece of plywood is a more recent option for the seat. Traditionally, slip seats were made as open frames that were upholstered with webbing, then stuffed with horsehair or hog's hair (or foam and batting), and covered with fabric. This is still done, but mostly on reproductions.

Determine the size of the seat blank by measuring the distance from the outsides of the rails from side to side, and from the front of the back rail to the front of the front rail. Add $\frac{1}{8}$ in. so that the seat blank will extend a little over the back rail. For this to happen, you will need to cut two small notches at the back of the seat blank for the legs. Leave about $\frac{1}{8}$ in. of space in front of and on the sides of the legs (see the slip seat detail in the drawing on p. 68). Cut out the seat, smooth all of the edges, and ease the corners a little.

I recommend attaching the seat to the chair with T-nuts and bolts. I used to attach seats with screws, but many years ago I had a customer whose daughter would lie down under the chairs and kick the seats off. Recently, I found my children under one of my older chairs, doing exactly the same thing. (How did they know?) The T-nuts are a little more trouble, but I've never had second thoughts about the switch.

Trace the corner block locations onto the bottom of the seat blank to locate the holes for attaching the seat.

Clamp the seat blank in place, then drill the holes to attach the seat. Keep the drill perpendicular (as best you can) to the seat blank.

UPHOLSTERING A SLIP SEAT

You may prefer to do the upholstery yourself. It's not hard to do, but it certainly isn't easy to do well. You need 1-in. foam, cotton or polyester batting (cotton is preferred, except for the most delicate fabrics, where some of the natural oils in the cotton batting might actually stain the fabric), a few upholstery tacks, and a heavy duty stapler in addition to your choice of fabric.

Lay a seat blank on the fabric, center it carefully on any pattern, and/or make sure the weave is straight (step 1). Then mark out the center both front and back on both fabric and on the underside of the seat blank. Keep in mind that working from the center out to the sides is basic to almost everything in upholstery. Cut out the fabric, leaving a 2-in. margin all around. Similarly, mark out and cut the foam and the batting flush with the seat blank.

Put the foam and batting on the seat blank, center the fabric over them, then turn the pile over (step 2). "Baste" the fabric into place with upholstery tacks at both front and rear centers. (It's called basting because the tacks are hammered only partway in and are removed later if you need to adjust the fabric.) Then stretch the fabric from side to side, and baste it into place at the centers of the sides (steps 3 and 4).

Step 1: *Align the center marks on the seat blank with the notches in the fabric.*

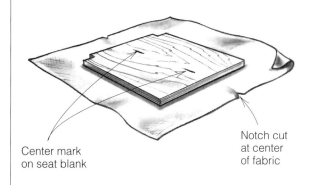

Center mark
on seat blank

Notch cut
at center
of fabric

Step 2: *Make a sandwich of the seat blank, foam, batting, and fabric.*

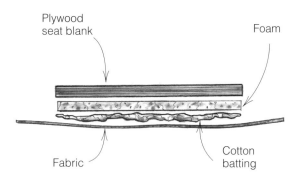

Plywood
seat blank

Foam

Fabric

Cotton
batting

To install the T-nuts, place the cut-out blank on the seat. From underneath, trace the corner blocks onto the bottom of the seat (see the top photo on p. 83). This will help to locate the holes for attaching the seat. The holes should wind up roughly centered on the corner blocks but, in any case, out of the way of the screws that attach the corner blocks. Drill holes in the seat blank with a 7/32-in. drill. Then reposition and clamp it on the chair, and drill down through the corner blocks (see the bottom photo on p. 83). Hammer 8-32 T-nuts into the holes in the seat blank from the top. Then counterbore the corner blocks from underneath with a 1/2-in. bit that leaves a flat-bottomed hole, deep enough for 8-32 by 2-in. or 2 1/2-in. machine screws with washers to reach the T-nuts.

Upholstering the seat

I send my seat blanks out to be upholstered. If you choose to do this as well, you will need to discuss what

Now, starting in the center of the front edge, work toward the corners, alternating from side to side and stretching and stapling the fabric into place (steps 5 and 6). Stretch carefully to keep the fabric straight and even. At the corners, you'll need to cut away some excess fabric, fold and tack from the side, then fold over and tack the front or back. Work the back the same way. Continue working your way around the sides, pulling and stapling on alternate sides as you go. Flip the seat over, and check for evenness constantly. Pull out the staples in any problem spots, adjust, and staple again.

It's a nice touch to staple some cambric to the underside of the seat. Cut holes through the cambric at the T-nut holes. Then attach the seat with the machine screws and washers.

Step 3: Pull the fabric tight and tack the center front and rear.

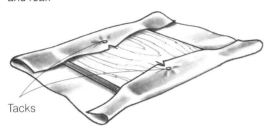

Tacks

Step 4: Tack the centers of the sides.

Step 5: Staple from the centers out, checking carefully to keep the fabric straight.

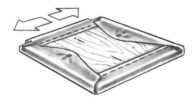

Step 6: Staple the sides in the same manner.

you want with your upholsterer. I usually get 1-in. foam and one layer of batting and ask for a rather flat look. This is simply my preference. Your upholsterer may have other suggestions. The choice of fabric is entirely up to you, but you should look for something that wears well; a fabric not designed for upholstery will wear out rather quickly on a chair seat. It also helps if the fabric has some texture; a completely smooth fabric is harder to work with. Stripes and plaids also make for more work because any variation from perfectly straight is instantly obvious. You will need about ¾ yard of fabric to cover two seats. Since upholstery fabric is usually 54 in. wide, you really can't buy for just one seat anyway.

Hammer glides into the bottoms of the legs, and have a seat. It's not quite the same experience in comfort as sitting in the completed dowel chair, but the accomplishment is much more significant.

5

CHILD'S
LADDER-BACK CHAIR

This is a fun chair to make and a really fun chair to give to a child. Children love having their own special chairs, and I have reports of customers' children who drag their chairs around with them from room to room. At his second birthday, I gave one to my son, who has seen me do a little bit of work on chairs. His immediate reaction was to fix it by turning it over to pound in some imaginary glides with his toy hammer. He also enjoyed sitting on it (and still does).

The Shaker ladder-back chair is probably the most familiar type of post-and-rung chair. Post-and-rung describes the overall structure: Round rungs join together two front and two rear posts, the rear posts support a back structure, and a seat is

woven around the seat rungs. The child's ladder-back chair is an offshoot of the Shaker chair style. This is not a reproduction, however, since I used ready-made hardwood dowels and no turning is necessary. And although I've added some simple design elements to this chair, it is still an easy chair to build. If you like, you can look for dimensioned drawings for an actual Shaker chair, from which parts could be turned to make a replica. The building process is the same, even though the details may differ.

As with the dowel chair, the ladder-back chair is made with round tenons for almost all of the joints (see the drawing on the facing page for dimensions on all parts). The structural design for the ladder-back chair is sound, as is the dowel chair,

but for slightly different reasons. There is some redundancy in that there are multiple joints on each side of the chair. But a bigger factor is that the structure is significantly reinforced by seat webbing, which prevents the rungs from pulling out of the posts.

The joinery on this chair consists mainly of drilling holes in the round leg posts, and inserting the dowels used for rungs. Getting the chair to fit together requires that those holes be drilled at the correct angles and in the proper locations. There are also mortises for the back slats, and these present a different challenge, as they're cut in the round stock.

This chair introduces the tapered or trapezoidal seat, although the joinery is so easy you might not even no-

CHILD'S LADDER-BACK CHAIR

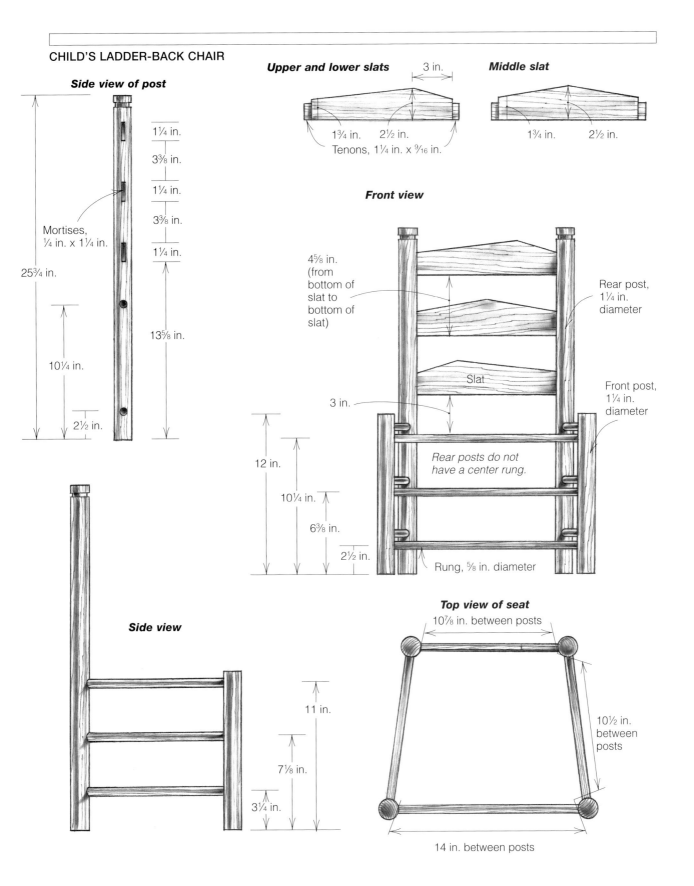

Side view of post

25¾ in.

1¼ in.
3⅜ in.
1¼ in.
3⅜ in.
1¼ in.

Mortises,
¼ in. x 1¼ in.

13⅝ in.

10¼ in.

2½ in.

Upper and lower slats

3 in.

1¾ in.   2½ in.
Tenons, 1¼ in. x ⁹⁄₁₆ in.

Middle slat

1¾ in.   2½ in.

Front view

4⅝ in.
(from
bottom of
slat to
bottom of
slat)

Slat

3 in.

Rear posts do not
have a center rung.

Rear post,
1¼ in.
diameter

Front post,
1¼ in.
diameter

12 in.

10¼ in.

6⅜ in.

2½ in.

Rung, ⅝ in. diameter

Side view

11 in.

7⅛ in.

3¼ in.

Top view of seat

10⅞ in. between posts

10½ in.
between
posts

14 in. between posts

The child's ladder-back chair on the left is the one the author made for his son.

tice that you're getting into one of the features that distinguishes most better chair designs. Many of these concepts will apply to the remaining chairs in the book.

INTRODUCING THE MASTER ANGLE

Chairs with seats that narrow toward the back have different angles at the front and at the back. But if you remember your geometry, you'll recall that these two angles are related: They add up to 180 degrees. What this means—even if you don't remember your geometry—is that we only have to worry about one angle in building a chair (at least until we get into compound angles). That is because one of the angles is a certain amount less than 90 degrees, and the other one is the same amount greater than 90 degrees. This difference between both of the angles and 90 degrees is what I call the "master" angle (see the top drawing on the

facing page). Knowing the master angle simplifies the joinery on this chair and just about every other chair because both front and rear joints can be cut using the same basic setups. On this chair, we will incorporate the master angle into a jig that controls the drilling angles.

MAKING THE DRILLING JIG

The jig for drilling the legs is very simple in concept, but there are a number of components that address what we need it to do (see the bottom drawing on the facing page).

First there is the support block. This holds the leg post securely so we can drill the necessary sets of holes for the rungs. To the support block we add a pair of indexing strips, which in conjunction with an indexing dowel inserted into one of the holes for the rungs, allows you to rotate the dowel and drill holes at exactly

FINDING THE MASTER ANGLE

Top view of seat

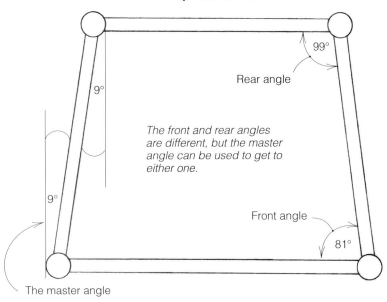

99°

Rear angle

9°

9°

9°

The front and rear angles are different, but the master angle can be used to get to either one.

Front angle

81°

The master angle

POST-DRILLING JIG

This jig slides along a low fence clamped to the drill press table. Note that the fence must be lower than the indexing strip.

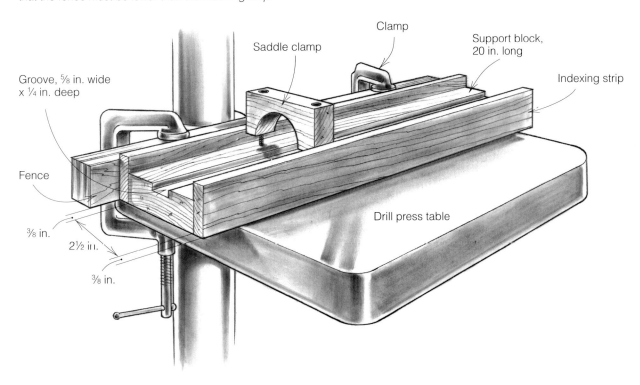

Clamp

Saddle clamp

Support block, 20 in. long

Indexing strip

Groove, ⅝ in. wide x ¼ in. deep

Fence

Drill press table

⅜ in.

2½ in.

⅜ in.

CHOOSING THE RIGHT DRILL BIT

What sort of drill bit should you use to drill the holes for the child's chair? The only real requirement is that the bit not have too long a point. The holes should be about ¾ in. deep, so any bit with a point longer than ½ in. should be avoided. Regular twist drills are also not very good because they tend to wander when starting the hole in a round dowel. I use a ⅝-in. brad point bit, mostly because it cuts quickly and cleanly. You should try test-fitting some of the dowels with the bit you intend to use. You may need to try out a few bits before you find something that is tight but within the range of shrinking to fit with hot sand (see "Cutting and fitting the rungs" on p. 95).

90 degrees to the first set of holes. We then incorporate the master angle by tilting the support block with a wedge, enabling us to drill holes at the necessary angles for both the front and back leg posts.

Making the support block

Start by making a support block 20 in. long with a trough down the middle for holding the dowel in place. I cut a ¼-in.-deep groove about ⅝ in. wide, although a V-groove the same width would work, too. Then make a saddle clamp—a block with holes for two screws on either side of a round notch cut to fit the dowel. Tightening the screws will hold the dowel firmly in place. You will also need a low fence, which will be clamped to the drill press table. The fence location is set to drill in the center of the dowel. Once set, it should allow you to drill all of the holes on that "side" of the dowel on center as the support block is moved back and forth along the fence. This is the basic jig; with a few additional refinements, it will help you to drill holes at the necessary angles for the putting this chair together.

Once you have the basic support block, the next step is to drill a centered ⅝-in. hole about ¾ in. deep in a length of 1¼-in. scrap dowel. How do you center the hole in the dowel? If you have a V-groove in the support block, you can align the point of the drill bit with the bottom of the V. If your groove is ⅝ in. wide, a centered drill bit should just touch both sides.

The easiest test is to actually drill and see that the hole begins symmetrically. Measuring with a dial calipers works, too, but only if the hole is deep enough. Adjust the location by moving the fence clamped to the drill press table in or out. When the

jig is set to drill on center, drill a hole in the dowel to the full ¾-in. depth.

Adding the indexing strips

The goal now is to be able to rotate the 1¼-in. dowel in either direction after drilling one hole and to be set up for drilling another hole at exactly 90 degrees to the first hole. Insert a 4-in. to 5-in. length of ⅝-in. scrap dowel into the hole just drilled in the center of the 1¼-in. dowel. (You may want to sand the end of the dowel a bit to make it easier to insert and remove from the hole.) I refer to this dowel as the indexing dowel.

Now rotate the larger dowel so that the indexing dowel is parallel with the base of the block. This is easy to do on a flat table. Measure the distance from the table surface to the bottom of the dowel to get a rough idea of the size strip needed. Then cut two strips to that width, and try them both close to the support block and out at the end of the dowel. Trim the strips (or recut them) until they both fit while the 1¼-in. dowel is held firmly or clamped to the support block (see the photo on the facing page). Then tack the two indexing strips onto the sides of the support block.

Once the strips are attached, check their accuracy by drilling holes at right angles in your scrap dowel, inserting lengths of ⅝-in. dowels, and checking the angle with a square. The square won't fit tight to both ⅝-in. dowels—the 1¼-in. dowel gets in the way—but you should be able to tell well enough if they are square. You don't need perfection. If the angle is greater than 90 degrees, add some tape to the top of the strip. If it is less than 90 degrees, you'll have to plane a little off the strips.

Determining the master angle

Now it's time to incorporate the master angle into the jig. Before you can do that, you need to know what that angle is. The easiest way to find this is to draw out the shape of the seat, and set a bevel gauge off the drawing (see the sidebar on p. 92). Drawing this at a drafting table is very easy, but an appropriately sized piece of ¼-in. plywood with a straight edge is what I use when my drafting table is covered with bills.

Once the seat shape is laid out on the plywood, set a bevel gauge to the front angle, and transfer this angle to the ends of a ¾-in.-thick scraps. The combination of the right angle at the end of the board and the rear (or front) angle will create the master angle (see the top drawing on p. 89). Cut out the wedges, clamp them together, and sand or plane them flush.

You might ask yourself why bother drawing the seat if you can just set the bevel gauge from a protractor? For this chair, the protractor isn't a bad idea, although the drawing gives you an angle that should be more accurate (not critical on this chair) and a clear picture of what the seat shape will be. You will need to use this procedure with any chair that you design or adapt.

Incorporating the master angle in the jig

Now that you know the master angle, you need to incorporate it into the jig. Start by raising up one side of the support block with the wedges—you need to hold the support block up at this angle to drill the holes for the rungs. To do this, I milled a scrap to the right thickness and tacked it to the bottom of the block (see the photo on p. 93). This involved a little trial-and-error fitting because the

Check the indexing strips to be sure they are the right width. The indexing dowel is touching both strips while in place on the support block, which indicates that the strips are correct.

LAYING OUT THE SEAT SHAPE

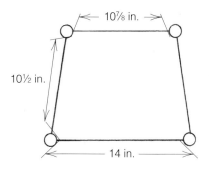

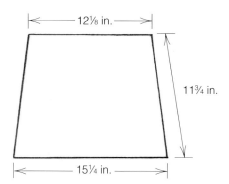

Step 1: To find the master angle, start by drawing the exact shape of the seat. In order to get accurate dimensions, it will help to get the posts out of the picture.

Step 2: To find the distances between the centers of the legs, just add 1¼ in. to the distances between the legs.

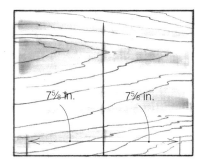

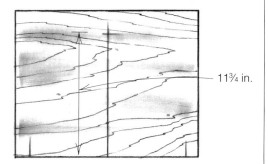

Step 3: Lay out the shape on paper or plywood, working from the center out. Start by drawing a center line, then draw in the base line.

Step 4: Next measure up the center line, and mark the center of the back of the chair.

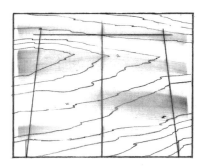

Step 5: Draw the line for the back of the chair parallel to the base line, and center it. Connect the ends of the back line and base line.

scrap actually rests on a corner set in from the back edge. Or you could attach the wedges to the bottom of the support block, and then attach a base (see the drawing below). If you are interested in making more chairs like this, you could hinge the support block on a base, and screw wedges of different angles into place as needed for different chairs.

The jig is now done, but you still need to reset the drill press fence to cut on center, reset the depth of cut, and check for accuracy. Drill a hole in a 1¼-in. piece of scrap dowel, then insert a ⅝-in.-diameter indexing dowel. Rotate the 1¼-in. dowel on the support block until the indexing dowel touches one of the strips on the side of the support block. Rotating "uphill" to the higher strip will set up to drill the acute angle on the

The completed drilling jig includes a support block, a saddle clamp, indexing strips, and a wedge milled to size to tilt the jig to the master angle.

TWO OTHER WAYS TO ADJUST THE JIG TO THE MASTER ANGLE

Attach all of these parts together with screws.

Saddle clamp

Indexing strip

Master angle wedge

Base

If you hinge the jig and base together, the jig can be used for different chairs depending on the wedge that is inserted.

Hinge

front leg posts; rotating "downhill" will create the obtuse angle necessary for the rear leg posts. (For this test, it doesn't matter which way you go.) Then drill a second hole. Insert another ⅝-in. dowel, and check the angle. Adjust if necessary by shimming or reworking the wedges. How important is accuracy in this chair? There is actually more of a margin for error than you might expect. The flexibility of the dowels allows for some misalignment, and you can always adjust the length of the front rails to compensate if your angles are really off.

PREPARING THE CHAIR PARTS

I make this chair with ready-made hardwood dowels—1¼-in. dowels for the leg posts and ⅝-in. dowels for the rungs. I usually use either cherry, walnut, or maple; these all finish up beautifully. However, the upper rungs should be straight-grained maple, ash, or oak for strength. Hardware store dowels are not really furniture quality and should be avoided on this project.

Drilling the leg posts

Cut the leg posts to length, then mark all four legs for the side rungs. A pencil line across the leg at the correct height is all that is needed, but try to keep all three of the lines on each leg on the same "side" of the post. Clamp the leg post into the support block making sure that all of the lines are visible, then drill the three holes. Unclamp, and drill the rest of the legs.

Next, mark the legs for the front and back rungs. (Note that there are only two rungs on the back.) Make sure you mark left and right front and rear legs correctly—they are all different. If you get confused, stand the legs up on a table roughly in position to remind yourself of what needs to be drilled where. This is similar to the "home position" I mentioned in Chapter 4 (see p. 74). Then insert an indexing dowel into one of the holes already in the leg. Place the leg into the support block. You will position each leg in the jig differently. For the front legs, the indexing dowel points uphill, and the top of the leg faces right for the right-hand leg (as seen from the front of the chair) and left for the left-hand leg (see the photo at left). For the rear legs, the indexing dowel points downhill, and the top of the leg is again to the left for the left-hand leg and to the right for the right-hand leg.

It's very easy to drill the wrong angle if you're not paying attention, so do a mental check before you start to drill, and take your time. The whole process is very quick, but it slows

This is the setup for drilling a left front leg. For the rear legs, the indexing dowel should face downhill. Note that once you've clamped the dowel in place, you can remove the indexing dowel if it gets in the way of the clamps.

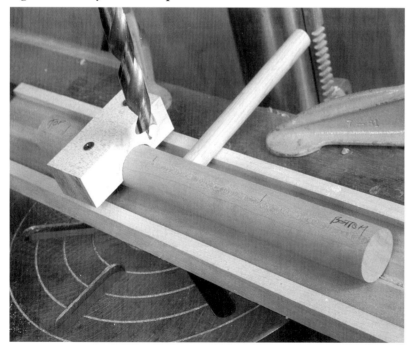

down considerably if you have to re-make legs. You may want to make a mark on the top of each leg prior to drilling to remind you where it goes. This is especially important if you are making more than one chair at a time.

Cutting and fitting the rungs

The next step is to determine the overall length for each of the rungs by adding the exact hole depths to the desired length between tenons. Cut the rungs for the back and sides to length from ⅝-in. dowel stock. If your angles are not quite what you had planned, you should wait to cut the front rungs until you've dry-assembled the rest of the chair so you can compensate.

You probably won't be able to fit the chair together well without shrink-ing the ends of the dowels. (If you can put it together, disassembly may be very hard, or it may be a sign that the holes are too big for the dowels.) As discussed in the sidebar on p. 63, shrink the dowel ends by leaving them standing in a can of hot sand for a couple of hours, then turn them over and repeat the process to shrink the opposite ends.

Dry-assemble the chair (or just the back and sides, if you need to mea-sure for the front rungs). Once all the rungs are in place and seated ful-ly, measure the actual distance (near-est point to nearest point) between the rear legs. You need this distance to make the back slats accurately. Then carefully disassemble the chair to work on the back slats.

Routing the mortises for the back slats

Even though the back-slat mortises are routed in a round dowel, the procedure is very similar to what we've done before with the mortis-ing block and square stock. The biggest difference is that you need to make two clamping blocks to hold the leg post securely in place for the mortising.

Setting up for mortising the leg posts. First, make the two clamp-ing blocks (see the drawing on p. 96). Then set the router fence so that the mortises will be centered on the leg posts. For this, you'll need to clamp a 1¼-in. scrap dowel in place on the mortising block. Measure out from the mortising block the dis-tance equal to half of the difference between the leg diameter and router bit diameter—in this case, 1¼ in. mi-nus ¼ in. divided by 2 = ½ in.—and make a mark on the scrap dowel. Set the router fence so that the near point of the router bit is just touch-ing the mark when the fence is tight against the mortising block. Set the depth of cut to about ⅝ in. with the router's depth stop.

Now make a very shallow test cut—just deep enough to have the router bit cutting a full path. Is the result a simple flat on the round leg, or is one side of the router bit cutting deeper? Adjust the fence to move the router in the direction of the deep side of the cut, if necessary.

Cutting the mortises. Mark the locations of the ends of each of the mortises with pencil lines (refer to the side view of post in the drawing on p. 87). Since there are six lines for the ends of the three mortises, you may find it helpful to make a mark between the lines to indicate just where to cut. Otherwise it's very easy to make a mistake and cut be-tween the mortises.

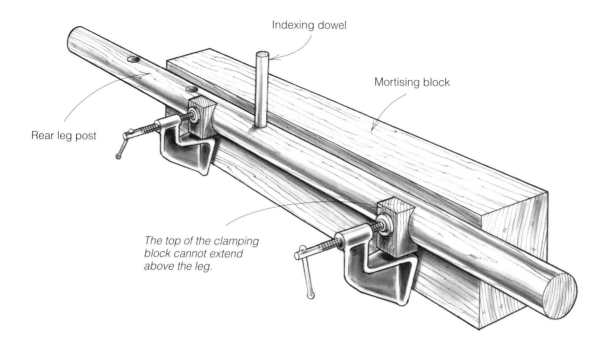

Indexing dowel

Mortising block

Rear leg post

*The top of the clamping
block cannot extend
above the leg.*

Clamp a rear leg post into your mortising block, and insert an indexing dowel into one of the side-to-side holes on the leg. To set up the leg flush with the top of the mortising block, align it with a board on top of the block, which extends out over the leg. To make sure the mortises are lined up exactly with the holes for the rungs, rotate the leg until the indexing dowel is square with the mortising block (see the photo on the facing page).

Cut the mortises by holding the fence securely against the mortising block and plunging in small increments as you move back and forth

between the marked lines. Raise the router up fully before stopping.

Making the back slats

On most Shaker chairs, the back slats were steam-bent to a gentle curve. On this chair, to keep things simple, we will cut the slats out of solid stock and leave them straight. Mill your stock to a little over ¼ in. thick so that when the slats are planed or sanded smooth, they will just fit into the leg mortises. Then rip the slats to 2½ in. wide. Add the combined mortise depths to the length between the rear legs measured earlier, and crosscut the slats to this length. The slats don't have full tenons—the sides extend right into the mortises—but top and bottom shoulders are still necessary. Cut these on the table-saw. Take great care to make the between-shoulder distance the same as the distance between the rear legs. Set the rip fence so the shoulders will equal the desired tenon length depth, and set the blade height to $\frac{1}{16}$ in. Cut the bottom shoulders on one side of each of the slats, cutting away all of the waste wood in a few quick passes, then raise the blade to $1\frac{3}{16}$ in., and cut the top shoulders on the same side of each of the slats. Now mark the desired distance between shoulders on one of the slats.

Before cutting the other shoulders, check to be sure the blade and the mark are in exactly the same place. Reset the fence, if necessary, and cut the remaining shoulders—first the top shoulders, then after resetting the blade height to $\frac{1}{16}$ in., the bottom shoulders. Lay out the design for the tops of the slats, and cut the slats to shape on the bandsaw. Smooth the edges and surfaces, and test the fit in the mortises.

Detailing the tops of the back legs

I wanted a distinctive detail on the tops of the rear leg posts, but one that didn't immediately suggest a Shaker-style pommel. The top detail I use on my production chairs is deceptively difficult (see the angled top and groove on the chair on the left in the photo on p. 88), and I couldn't think of a way to do it without some fancy jigging and machinery. But the top for this chair is easy. Lower the blade on the tablesaw to cut $\frac{1}{8}$ in. deep. Then set a stop on the miter gauge so that the blade will cut a slot $\frac{5}{8}$ in. from the top of the leg. Hold the leg against the miter gauge with the bottom against the stop block, and advance into the saw

When setting up to cut mortises in the legs for the back slats, make sure that the indexing dowel is at 90 degrees to and the post is flush with the top of the mortising block.

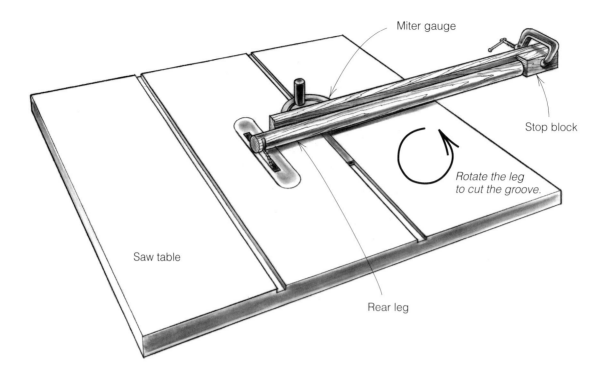

Miter gauge

Stop block

Rotate the leg
to cut the groove.

Saw table

Rear leg

blade. When the leg is over the center of the blade, slowly and securely rotate the leg against the rotation of the blade until a kerf is cut all the way around (see the drawing above). Always hold the leg securely, and rotate it from the bottom forward (against the rotation of the blade). Then push clear of the blade with the miter gauge, shut down, and remove the leg. To finish the top detail, chamfer the top edge with some sandpaper. Chamfer the tops of the front legs to match.

Sanding the chair parts

This is by far the easiest chair to smooth in preparation for gluing up and finishing. Sand all of the leg posts lightly with sandpaper. Sand

the rungs, too, but avoid the ends so you don't loosen the fit in the legs. Lightly chamfer the back slats. Then get ready to put the chair together.

ASSEMBLING THE CHAIR

To assemble the chair, you'll need a slow-setting glue (white glue is best), glue spreaders made from a short piece of 3/8-in. dowel and a thin flat stick, clamps, and clamp pads. Then lay out the chair parts. Sort through to find the least attractive ones to put in the top holes, where they will be covered by the woven seat. The rungs for the back and the sides look like they are interchangeable. They are not, so set them apart before they get mixed together.

As with most chairs, the glue-up for this one is best done in stages. Assemble the front and back of the chair first.

Gluing up the back

On the back it should be immediately obvious which set of holes you need to use—the ones in line with the mortises. Spread glue in the mortises and holes, but not on the ends of the rungs because the risk of squeeze-out is too great. If the dowels have been shrunk enough, the fit shouldn't be so tight that all of the glue is squeezed to the bottom. If the dowels haven't been shrunk enough, you may need to reshrink and sand again.

Insert the slats and rungs into one side, then work on getting everything in place on the other side. Use the same strategy used in assembling the dowel chair: Start at one end and work one piece into place at a time. Put a clamp on the end you started with to keep it from popping out. Add a clamp to the other side, and tighten as you get each piece in its place. Add another clamp or two to clamp everything up tight. Once you've clamped the back up tight, you need to check for twist. Unclamp, and lay the assembly down on a flat surface. If it does not lie flat, twist it back to flat if this is still possible. Don't force it, though. Some of the twist will be pulled out in final assembly.

Gluing up the front

On the front, it's easy to get confused about which holes to use. Check to be sure you spread glue in the lower set of holes. (Make sure you know which is the top, too!) Insert the dowels, then clamp together. Check for twist as you did with the back assembly.

The final assembly

The final assembly is a bit unnerving. When you insert all of the side rungs in the front leg posts, the opposite ends of these rungs are not spaced right to fit in the holes in the back leg posts. They are spaced correctly for the bottoms of the holes, but not for the tops, which is where you need to put them right now. Insert the rungs into one side, then pull gently on the rungs until they fit into the other side holes. Clamp the chair together evenly with at least four clamps. Clamp the middle rungs, with the pressure from above and below, if they aren't seating.

THE FINISHING TOUCHES

It's almost a chair. But there is still plenty to do between applying the finish and weaving the seat.

Applying finish to the chair

Finish the chair with oil and wax. Refer to the appendix (see p. 195) for a discussion of how to get excellent results with this finish. Or use your own preferred finish. When the finish is dry, you can move on to weaving the seat.

Weaving the seat

There are numerous options for weaving the seat on a post-and-rung chair: fabric tape, nylon webbing, cane, rush, or wood splint. The most common material for a woven seat like this is fabric tape, which is available through a number of places that specialize in Shaker furniture reproductions and through good fabric stores. The fabric tape is easy to do and looks great. It is also more durable than the other options.

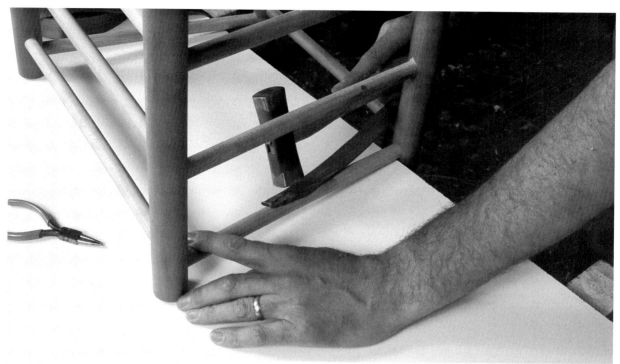

Start the warp on the bottom of the seat on one side. Note that the chair is upside down on the work surface here.

For this chair, I like nylon webbing—either a solid webbing or a hollow webbing (a flattened tube)—which is available through camping supply stores. The nylon webbing is incredibly strong (especially the hollow stuff) and is available in really bright colors. I think it's perfect for this chair, and it's what I used in the chairs in the photos. I chose 1-in.-wide webbing, but ½-in. and ⅝-in. webbing are available, too. These look great as well. They are about twice as much work, however, and you'll need about twice as much.

To weave a seat for this chair, you'll need 30 ft. of 1-in.-wide tape or webbing for the warp–the part that you wrap around the seat rungs from front to back–and 27 ft. for the weft–the part you weave through the warp from side to side. If you are going to use two colors, the warp is usually the darker color. You'll also need a few upholstery tacks (or sta-

ples and a heavy-duty stapler), possibly a needle and thread if you don't have long enough lengths of webbing, and a piece of 1-in.-thick foam rubber large enough to fit just inside the seat opening.

If you need to splice together sections of webbing or fabric tape, arrange to do this on the bottom side of the chair. Overlap the old and new pieces for about 3 in., and sew them together using the needle and thread.

Weaving the warp Start by attaching an end of the warp in the middle of the underside of one of the side seat rungs using a couple of upholstery tacks or a staple (see the photo above). Then bring the webbing up around the back rung, across the top of the chair, and down around the front rung. Wrap the webbing until about a third of the seat is wrapped, then insert the 1-in. foam into the space between the up-

Insert the foam with the warp partially wrapped around the rungs.

per and lower webbing (see the photo above). Continue wrapping until the back rung is filled; then wrap once more around the front, and tack to the middle of the other side rung. The warp should be taut but not tight—no slack, but not pulling in on the rungs either. Cut off the webbing at an angle. If you're using nylon webbing, you should melt the ends a little with a cigarette lighter or soldering iron to keep the web-

bing from unraveling. Be careful not to burn yourself or the chair with either the heat source *or* the molten webbing.

Since the chair is wider at the front than it is in the back, you still need to fill in the two open triangles on the sides toward the front. Tack a piece of webbing near the back or the underside of the side rung, bring it up over the front rung, and attach it

COPING WITH ALL THE WEBBING

So how do you deal with 9 yards of tape or webbing? With the warp, it's easy. Coil it up into a roll, and just keep passing the roll over and under the rungs. It may get twisted up a bit, but it's easy to straighten out. The weft is much more of a challenge. The best solution I've found is to ignore the end of the webbing. Instead, to begin each new row, fold over the webbing about 18 in. away from the chair, and weave the folded-over loop through the warp (see the drawing at right). Then pull all the rest of the webbing through.

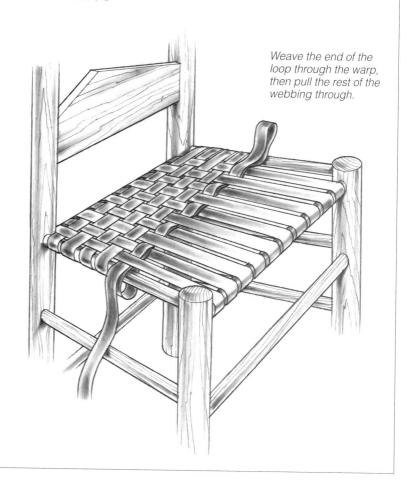

Weave the end of the loop through the warp, then pull the rest of the webbing through.

toward the back on the top side of the same rung. I usually try to tack to the inside of the rung, so a bump doesn't show through the webbing. Do the same on the other side. This completes the warp.

Weaving the weft Turn the chair over, and insert one end of the webbing underneath the warp in the middle at the rear rung. Spread the warp apart, and tack the end to the rung. Then weave over one row of warp and under the next until you get to a side rail. Turn the chair over,

and begin weaving across the top. Continue weaving both top and bottom, making sure you weave the opposite way from the row before (see the photo on the facing page). You don't want two "overs" or "unders" to be next to each other, unless you are intentionally weaving a different pattern. Keep pushing the new rows of weft toward the back of the chair, tight against the previous rows.

Weaving gets more and more difficult as you get closer to the front rung (although there is less of the

Weave rows so that no two "overs" or "unders" are next to each other.

webbing to deal with). Try using a thin, smooth stick (like a tongue depressor) to push doubled-over webbing through the warp, or use needle-nosed pliers or surgical forceps to try to pull it through. I always find this to be tough on my fingers, especially in the winter when my skin is dry to begin with. Taping your fingertips is not a bad idea.

After weaving the last row on top of the chair, you still have half a row on the bottom to weave so that you can tack the end of the webbing to the underside of the middle of the front rung. You'll have to work hard at spreading the warp apart to attach the webbing there, and then work to cover the end back up once it is tacked into place. While the chair is still upside down, hammer the glides to the bottoms of the legs.

Turn the chair back over, and even out the woven seat, pushing and pulling until it looks even. Go ahead and sit down. A low chair is actually nice for certain types of work around the shop. With your knees up, the straight back feels pretty good. But the chair isn't for you—it's a gift for someone, isn't it?

6
SLAT-BACK CHAIR

So far, we have danced around the complexities of joined chairs. The right-angle chair had mortise-and-tenon joints, but no angles to contend with. The child's ladder-back chair had angles, but no mortise-and-tenon joinery. With the slat-back chair, we finally get to the heart of chairmaking: joinery with angles. This chair is important for more than its angled joinery, however. In its design and structure as well as in the skills and techniques we'll develop to build it, the slat-back chair provides the foundation for a multitude of other chair designs.

This chair introduces features we haven't looked into yet: more completely shaped rear legs, a seat and side rails that tilt back slightly, and slats that tilt back. In addition, the seat is trapezoidal: the chair back is narrower than the front (see the drawing on p. 106 for dimensions on parts). Before worrying too much about all of these apparent complications, we'll look at some very interesting things we can do to simplify construction.

Let's start with a mental exercise. Imagine that we are looking at a chair built with only right angles (see the drawing on p. 107). Cut a little bit off the rear legs, and the chair tilts back a little. Now imagine that the rear legs are made from wider boards. Out of these wider boards, we can cut the legs into a variety of shapes without changing the joinery at all. Cutting legs out this way is a simple, effective approach. But it does waste wood, especially if you're making more than one chair. And occasionally, it may not be possible to fit the leg you want on a given board because you have to align the middle of the leg with an edge of the board. However, this concept is very useful even if it isn't always put into practice. If we shift our perspective a little, we see that the critical part of the slat-back chair (and of most joined chairs) from a construction standpoint is actually the flat area on the front of the rear leg where the side rail joins the leg. This is all that remains of the edge of the wide board from which the legs are cut. The shoulders of the side rail tenon seats against this flat. And the angle of this flat relative to the upper and lower part of the rear leg determines how and if the whole chair

SLAT-BACK CHAIR

Front view

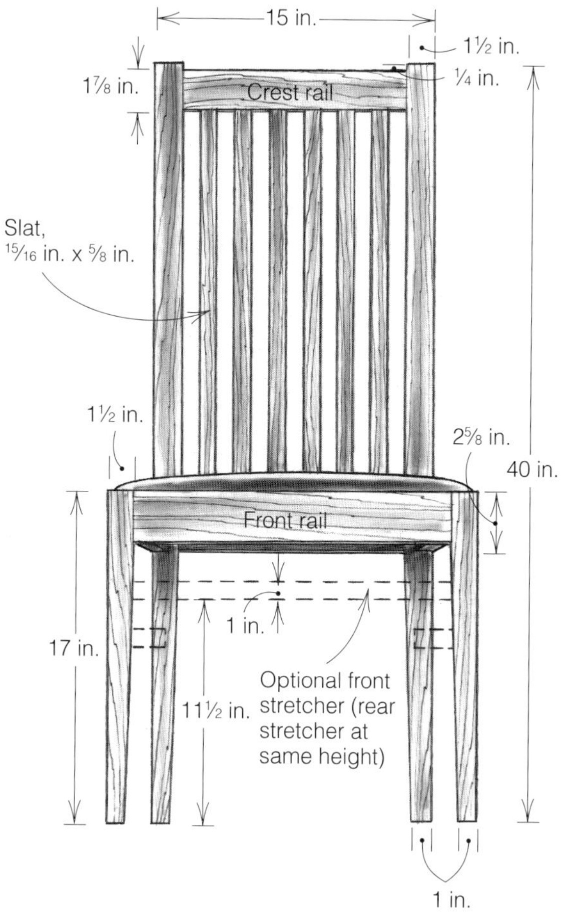

15 in.

1½ in.

¼ in.

1⅞ in.

Crest rail

Slat,
¹⁵⁄₁₆ in. x ⅝ in.

1½ in.

2⅝ in.

40 in.

Front rail

17 in.

1 in.

Optional front
stretcher (rear
stretcher at
same height)

11½ in.

1 in.

Side view

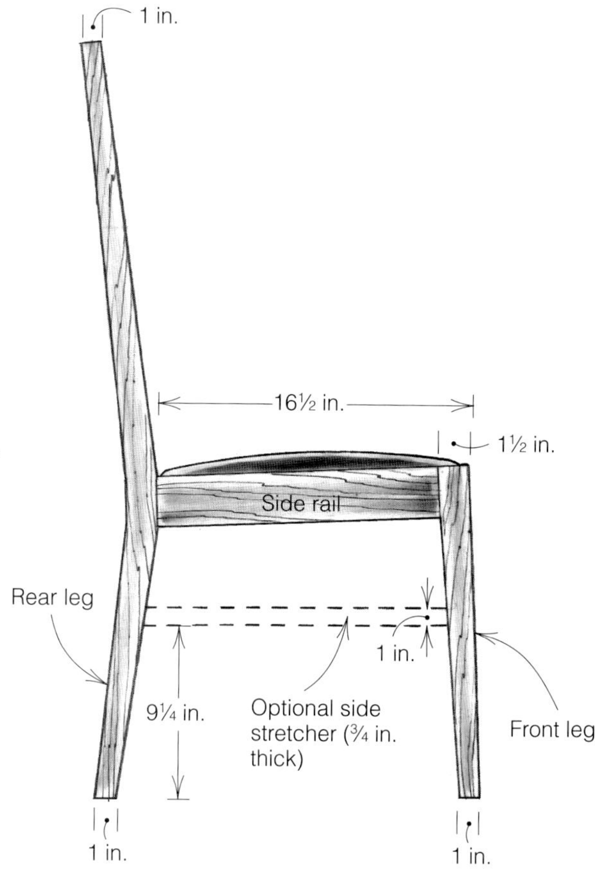

1 in.

16½ in.

1½ in.

Side rail

Rear leg

9¼ in.

1 in.

Optional side
stretcher (¾ in.
thick)

Front leg

1 in.

1 in.

Top view

15 in.

16½ in.

Corner block,
1⅛ in. x 2¼ in. x
about 5½ in.

20 in.

Rail detail

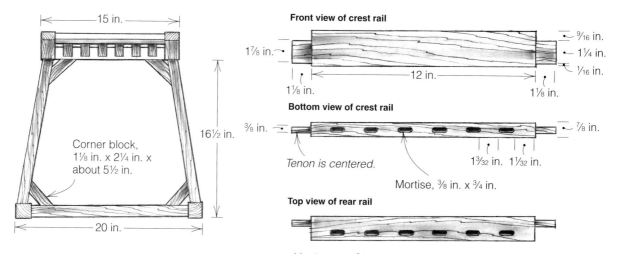

Front view of crest rail

1⅞ in.

9⁄₁₆ in.

1¼ in.

¹⁄₁₆ in.

12 in.

1⅛ in.

1⅛ in.

Bottom view of crest rail

⅜ in.

⅞ in.

Tenon is centered.

1³⁄₃₂ in.   1¹⁄₃₂ in.

Mortise, ⅜ in. x ¾ in.

Top view of rear rail

*Mortises are ⁵⁄₁₆ in. back from the front edge, the
same distance as on the crest rail.*

Side view of chair with only right angles

The same right-angled chair tipped back a little bit

The same chair with a wider rear leg

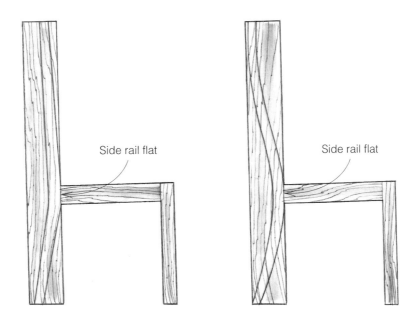

Side rail flat

Side rail flat

As long as you maintain the side rail flat, a variety of leg shapes can be cut from the wide rear leg.

REAR LEG PATTERN AND MORTISE LAYOUTS

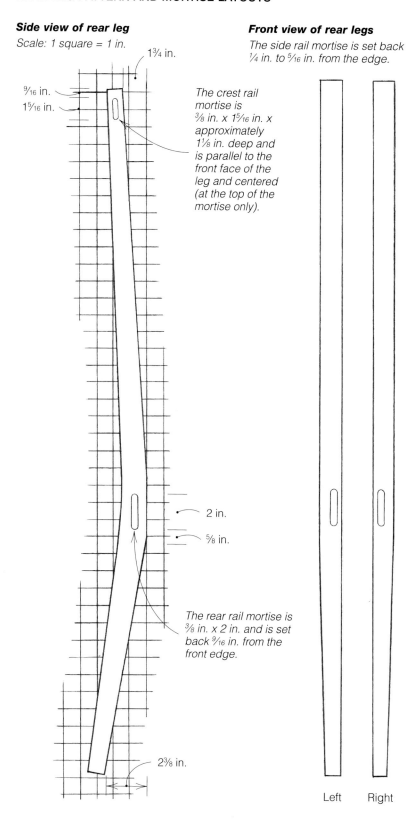

Side view of rear leg

Scale: 1 square = 1 in.

9/16 in.

1 5/16 in.

1 3/4 in.

The crest rail mortise is 3/8 in. x 1 5/16 in. x approximately 1 1/8 in. deep and is parallel to the front face of the leg and centered (at the top of the mortise only).

2 in.

5/8 in.

The rear rail mortise is 3/8 in. x 2 in. and is set back 9/16 in. from the front edge.

2 3/8 in.

Front view of rear legs

The side rail mortise is set back 1/4 in. to 5/16 in. from the edge.

Left   Right

will go together. The side rail flats are our reference surfaces; they are where we will begin the joinery on this chair, and they will be the foundation of many of the chairs to come.

Note that we take a different approach to joinery from that of a right-angle chair. The joinery is different on the front and rear legs, so we set up and work on each individually.

MAKING THE REAR LEGS

The work on the slat-back chair begins with the rear legs. Start by making up a full-size pattern in 1/4-in. plywood (see the drawing at left). Not surprisingly, it is helpful to lay out and cut the pattern with the side rail flat aligned with the edge of the board from which the pattern will be cut. Once the pattern is cut, sand the edges smooth, and work on getting the curve of the back even and graceful. Then trace the pattern onto the wood you've chosen for the rear legs, which has been planed to the proper thickness.

Now you have to make a significant decision. If the wood cooperates, you may want to cut the legs as described previously, with the side rail flats aligned with the jointed edges of the board(s). If this does not work or if you would rather not waste quite so much wood, there are a few extra steps involved. Even if you decide to take the simpler approach, (see "Cutting rear legs from the middle of a board" on p. 110), I suggest that you read through these extra steps anyway, as they are critical to other chair designs.

Aligning the side rail flats with an edge

Aligning the flats with an edge greatly simplifies the joinery because the mortises for both the side rail and rear rail tenons can be cut while the board is still square. Start by laying out a left and a right leg as mirror opposites. That way you don't need to do additional work to locate a mortise on the unmarked side of the board. Be very careful to line up the side rail flat on the leg pattern exactly with the edge of the board. Since the side rail flat is a very short part of a long leg, errors are easily introduced. Any error will be greatly magnified and will create significant problems later. Clamp a piece of scrap as a fence to the edge of the board, and carefully butt the side rail flat against it. Measure back from the edge of the board to the top of the pattern to be sure the alignment is the same.

Now lay out the rear and side rail mortises. Lay out the rear rail mortises first (see the drawing on the facing page), then transfer the lines around for the side rail mortises. This avoids having to measure up the angled leg. Locate the side rail mortises about 1/4 in. to 5/16 in. from the outside of the legs to allow room for the rear rail tenons. These are joints that are subject to a great deal of stress, so it is best to cut the mortises to within 1/4 in. of the back of the legs. Use a mortising block to cut these (see the sidebar on p. 43). Rear rail mortises are located 9/16 in. back from the front edge of the leg. Make them as deep as possible without cutting through into the side rail mortises.

Cutting the mortises is as simple as setting the fence on a plunge router for the proper distance and routing to the marked lines. A jig isn't really necessary because the board is wide enough to easily support the router.

Bandsaw the legs, then smooth the bandsawn edges. (The cutoffs will come in handy later as sanding blocks.) Planing the longer surfaces on the front of the legs can be done by hand or carefully on the jointer if you've cut well to the outside of your lines when bandsawing. Be certain to leave enough of the side rail flats for the side rails to seat against!

The backs of the legs are planed, scraped, and sanded, as necessary. A compass plane—a plane with an adjustable curved sole—is a help with the curves, but a surprising amount of wood can be planed with an ordinary smooth plane skewed at a steep angle. A sanding block curved to match the curve of the leg backs works well and might be found in your scrap bin. Or use a cutoff saved from bandsawing earlier. Just trim and smooth a 6-in. section from the curved part of one of the leg cutoffs. Holding the legs in a bench vise for planing, scraping, and sanding can be made a little easier if you place a block the same thickness as the leg at the bottom of the vise while clamping up the leg—this evens out the pressure that the vise exerts.

Cutting the crest rail mortises completes the rear leg joinery. Keep the tops of the mortises as far away from the tops of the legs as possible (still keeping the rail location where it should be, that is) to help prevent splitting. If you offset the crest rail tenons toward the bottom of the rail, there will be a little more space available above the mortises without changing the location of the rail.

This is similar to how we've been offsetting the joints on front legs to the bottoms of the rails in previous chapters. I would also suggest making the crest rail mortises about 1/16 in. longer than the tenons will be. This can help later when fitting the slats (see "Tenoning the slats" on p. 121). Taper the inside faces of the lower rear legs, if you wish.

Cutting rear legs from the middle of a board

It's surprising how often it doesn't work to cut the legs with the side rail flats aligned with the edges: Knots get in the way, the grain pattern doesn't look right, or the board you want to use works only if you angle the leg a little. It is also surprising just how many more legs you can get out of a board when they are "nested"—a big factor when making a set of chairs. Whatever the reason, when cutting rear legs from the middle of a board, the side rail flats must be flattened and positioned accurately after the legs are cut out. In many respects, you should still treat the side rail flats as if they were the straight edge of a board. The payoff is that this makes the joinery much more manageable.

Start by laying out the legs and bandsawing them to shape. Then plane,

A SHOOTING BOARD FOR PLANING THE SIDE RAIL FLAT

Keep the back of the plane solidly on the support block at all times when planing the side rail flat.

Clamp

Side rail flat

Block to support plane

Registration block

Rear leg

¼-in. plywood board for aligning the legs accurately

Plane

Clamp

Registration block

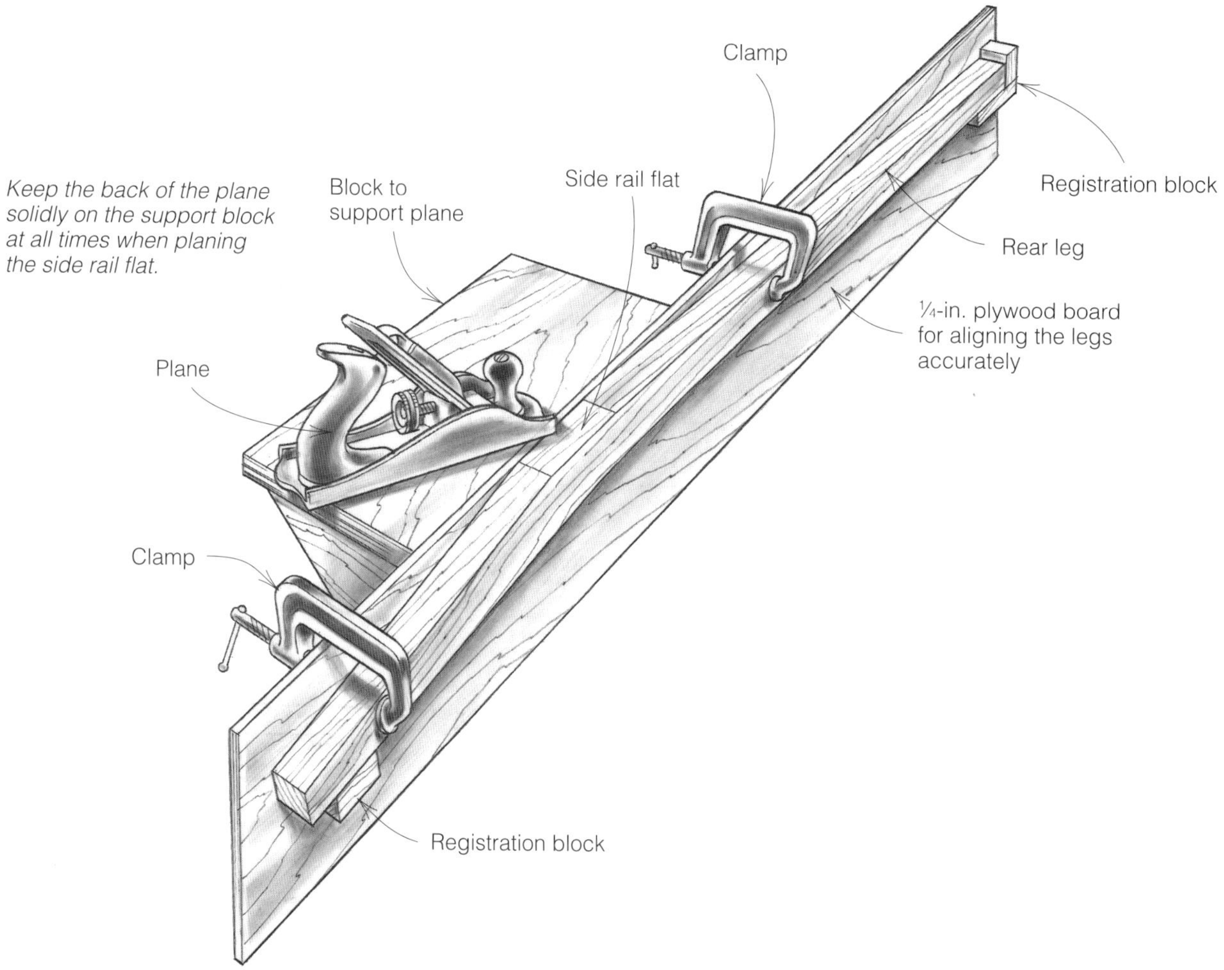

scrape, and sand smooth, as described on p. 109, leaving the side rail flats rough for now. There are a few approaches to getting the flats just right. It is possible to hand-plane them very carefully, but I prefer to make a simple shooting board, which makes it easier to control both the position of the side rail flat relative to the rest of the leg and to ensure its flatness (see the drawing on the facing page). While the leg is still clamped to the shooting board, the side rail mortise can be routed using a plunge router with a fence—in the same way the mortising block is used. Note, too, that the shooting board can be used for other chair designs by simply drawing new leg profiles and moving the registration blocks.

However you cut the flats, check the results by resting the legs in pairs on their side rail flats on a flat surface. If the tops and bottoms of the legs don't line up, rework the flats until they do. If the legs are just slightly off, it may be easier to plane the tops and/or bottoms of one or both of the legs so that they line up rather than messing with the flats.

Mortising the inner sides of the rear legs for the rear rail is next. The side rail flats are again our main point of reference. This is important to keeping the legs in alignment. Clamp the side rail flat to the side of the mortising block or even to a thick board that is long enough for the router fence to ride on. Cut these mortises as deep as possible without going through into the side rail mortises. Then cut the crest rail mortises with the mortising block and plunge router.

Now we're at the same place we ended up when using the other method. Taper the inside faces of the lower rear legs, if you wish.

MAKING THE FRONT LEGS

Cut the front legs to size, then lay out the intersecting mortises (see the drawing below). Once the mortises are cut, you can taper the legs. This is in keeping with the concept of cutting joints in square stock whenever possible. Taper only the inside faces—the ones that have mortises in them. Start the tapers about 3 in. down from the top. Be careful not to creep up into the area where the rails will seat.

INTERSECTING MORTISES ON FRONT LEGS

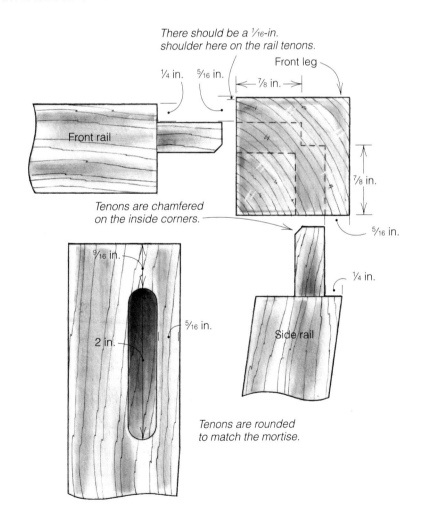

There should be a 1/16-in. shoulder here on the rail tenons.

Front leg

1/4 in.   5/16 in.   7/8 in.

Front rail

7/8 in.

5/16 in.

Tenons are chamfered on the inside corners.

9/16 in.

2 in.

5/16 in.

1/4 in.

Side rail

Tenons are rounded to match the mortise.

MAKING THE RAILS

Mill the rail stock to 1⅛ in. thick, or just use surfaced 5/4 stock, which will be 1¹⁄₁₆ in. thick. Cut the rails to width, but leave them long for now.

Cutting straight tenons

With the tenons, we start with the easy stuff, but not just because it's easy. We need to get the front and back of the chair together temporarily to accurately determine the angles for the tenons on the side rails. Cut the straight tenons on the front and rear rails, and cut the crest rail tenons as well. The ends of the front rail tenons (and the front tenons on the side rails) need to be mitered since the mortises intersect. If you're making a set of chairs, it may pay to cut joints in only one of the front rails now. The front rail is where you can correct for errors in the angle of the side rails. Remaking one is a whole lot easier than remaking six.

Cutting mortises

Cut the ⅜-in. by ¾-in.-long mortises for the slats in the top of the rear rail and the bottom of the crest rail at this time (see the Rail detail in the drawing on p. 106). Lay out the mortises, then set up the rails in the mortising block to cut them. Cut the crest rail mortises first, centered on the thickness of the rail. Then cut the rear rail mortises ⁵⁄₁₆ in. back from the front face. If you place the front faces of the rails against the mortising block, this will follow automatically.

Dry-assemble the front legs with the front rail in place and the rear legs with the rear and crest rails in place, and clamp them tight.

Cutting angled tenons

Why don't I give exact angles for the side rail tenons? Partly because angles add unnecessarily to the feeling that chairs are very complicated. But also because there are numerous opportunities for error in reading angles and setting tools by angle scales. I find measured angles useful (though not necessary) for creating full-size drawings, but there are plenty of places to stray from the drawings when building a chair—some of them intentional. I change plans often when going through the design stage on my chairs because they are harder than most pieces to figure out on paper. I would much rather get angles off a chair in progress, using a bevel gauge. I hardly ever use a protractor. Instead, I use the bevel gauge setting to make a wedge for holding a piece at a particular angle while I'm working on it or to set up a tool.

For the chair to fit together, both the angle and the length of the side rails must be determined accurately. (Although in a pinch, you could go back and change the front rail length to fit, as I mentioned earlier.) Then the side rails must be cut to length and the joints carefully marked. Finally, the tenons are cut and fit to the mortises. All of this—even cutting the rails to length—is a little different from straight tenon work. Since we are exploring what is likely to be new territory, I will go into each step in a little more detail.

Deciding the side rail length

The length of the side rails between the tenons is a design decision, based on how deep you want the chair to be overall. For this chair, I've set this measurement at 15⁵⁄₁₆ in. because I wanted the depth of the chair to be 16½ in. from the front of the rear rail to the front of the front rail.

Determining the side rail angle

There are two methods I use to figure out the angle for the side rail. I take the angle either off a full-scale drawing or from the actual sub-assemblies held in place with a positioning jig. Which method you choose will probably depend on whether or not you plan to make other chair designs (or on how much of a jig fanatic you are). Working from a drawing is fairly simple. If you draw on a piece of ½-in. plywood with a straight edge, you can set a bevel gauge right from the drawing. And as a bonus, you can use the plywood for a seat blank (see the sidebar below for how to obtain the side rail angle this way).

OBTAINING THE SIDE RAIL ANGLE

Follow these steps and refer to the drawing at right to create a half-plan view of the chair to get the side rail angle.

Step 1: *Measure the front and rear leg assemblies while they are clamped up for a dry fit. The only important measurements are the overall widths at rail height between front legs and between rear legs.*

Step 2: *Mark a center point on the base line (the flat edge of the plywood), and draw a perpendicular centerline up from it, about 15 in. long.*

Step 3: *On the base line, measure over exactly half the width of the rear leg assembly, and mark the rear leg point.*

Step 4: *Draw a line 15 in. up and parallel to the base line. This line is at the proper seat depth for this chair.*

Step 5: *Locate the front leg point on the upper line by measuring over from the centerline half the measured width of the front leg assembly.*

Step 6: *Connect the front and rear leg points to get both the angle and the length between tenons of the side rails.*

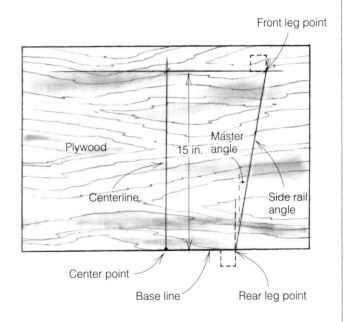

What you've drawn is actually half of a plan view of the chair between the front and rear legs. This provides just enough information to work with. As I discussed in Chapter 5, the angle we really need is the "master" angle—the angle from which we can create either the front or the back angle. This angle is the difference between either the front or the back angle and 90 degrees. Drawing a perpendicular line up from the rear leg point creates it. Or, a bevel gauge can be used in conjunction with a square to get the angle. Since this comes up fairly often in chairmaking, I have made a "bevel square" that combines both tools in one and reads the master angle directly (see the drawing below).

Because the drawing method is not very flexible when I want to experiment with a new design or need to change something on a standard design, I have built an adjustable positioning jig that helps hold the front and rear subassemblies in alignment and the desired distance apart while I copy angles with the bevel square or bevel gauge (see the drawing on the facing page). The jig allows me to quickly and easily experiment with the seat depth (see the left photo on the facing page). And I like getting the angle right off the chair.

Mark the centers of the front and rear rails first, then clamp on the respective halves of the jig, carefully lining up the center marks and lining up the jig flush with the top of the rails. Then slide the two halves of the jig together, and clamp at the desired distance—in this case, with the inside of the front rail 15¼ in. from the inside of the rear rail. The bevel square easily copies the master angle (see the right photo on the facing page).

Once you have the master angle, cut a wedge for tilting the rails while cutting and tenoning; it will wind up roughly ¼ in. thick at one end, 1¾ in. thick at the other end, and 8¾ in. long. It is an excellent idea to test out the angle on a pair of test sticks made of ¾-in. stock before cutting and fitting the joints in your side-rail stock. Using the wedge, cut the test sticks to the between-tenon length—15⁵⁄₁₆ in. They do not need tenons. As you will do when cutting tenons, cut one end of the stick with one side down on the wedge, then flip the piece, and cut the other end with the other side down. The ends

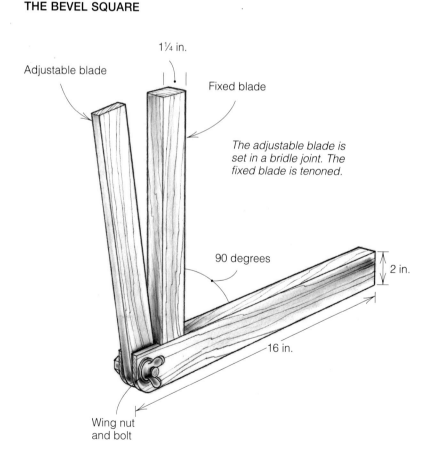

THE BEVEL SQUARE

Adjustable blade

1¼ in.

Fixed blade

The adjustable blade is set in a bridle joint. The fixed blade is tenoned.

90 degrees

2 in.

16 in.

Wing nut and bolt

To help determine the side rail angles, the positioning jig is clamped on the dry-assembled front and rear leg units. We get a little early gratification because it does look a little like a chair at this stage.

With the positioning jig holding the chair front and back in place, I can obtain the side rail angle and the master angle with my shopmade bevel square.

THE ADJUSTABLE POSITIONING JIG

Center mark

10 in.

2 in.

Clamp to hold together at the proper distance

Clamp to front rail

Guide strip

2¾ in.

2¾ in.

1 in.

Clamp to rear rail

1 in.

Screwed or tenoned to crosspiece at 90 degrees

15½ in.

The center mark is aligned with the mark at the center of the front rail.

2 in.

MARKING ANGLED TENONS

Follow the steps outlined in the photos below to simplify marking out your angled tenons on the rails.

Step 1: Begin the process of cutting one end of the rail at an angle. Use the master angle wedge to tilt the workpiece, and leave the saw blade at 90 degrees. Hold the rail and wedge firmly against the miter gauge.

Step 2: Mark the shoulder line parallel to the angled end. This distance from the end of the rail should be the length of the tenon; measure this perpendicular to the end of the rail, not along the edge. Now mark the shoulder at the other end of the rail, then add the tenon length, as measured perpendicular to the shoulder. This gives the overall length of the rail. Cut to length with the wedge.

Step 4: Transfer the marks down to the shoulder line. Use a marking gauge, or draw the lines parallel to the edge using your fingers as a guide.

Step 5: Transfer the lines back up to the end of the rail, perpendicular to the end. These are now the actual tenon layout lines.

Step 3: Mark the tenon on the end. This is not an actual location for the tenon. Instead you are marking the end of the rail as if it were the shoulder, seated against the leg. You can either measure the mortise location, adjust for the 1/16 in. that the rail is set in from the edge of the leg (both front and rear), and mark it out on an edge at the end of the rail, or you can hold the rail up to the leg and transfer the mortise location.

Step 6: Bring the lines from the edge across the end of the rail. These are the actual layout lines for the tenons.

DETERMINING THE RAIL LENGTH AND SHOULDER LOCATIONS

Step 1. Cut one end at an angle.

Step 2. Draw the shoulder line parallel to the end.

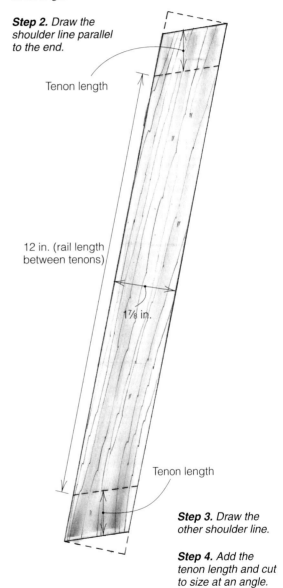

Tenon length

12 in. (rail length between tenons)

1⅞ in.

Tenon length

Step 3. Draw the other shoulder line.

Step 4. Add the tenon length and cut to size at an angle.

I'm routing an angled tenon with the tenoning jig. The wedge is in place between the rail and the jig. Here I'm using a shorter jig and the rail is clamped in the vise, but this isn't necessary.

should be parallel. Check the fit by clamping the test sticks into place between the front and rear sub-assemblies while they are still held in place by the positioning jig (or enlist some help for this). Adjust the wedge, if necessary, by adding tape or by planing (or even recutting).

Marking out the tenons It seems natural to cut the rails to length now, but there is a problem. We know the length between tenons and the tenon lengths, but the tenons are at an angle, so we can't just add everything together. We could leave the rails a little long, but then it becomes a problem locating the tenons exactly. The joint is usually marked out and cut based on the end of the tenon, but it fits together with the shoulder tight against the leg. Instead, we will combine cutting and marking out the tenons, at least for the first rail. We will then have the necessary length and can use the first rail to set up machines or jigs for cutting the tenons. Believe me, this all sounds much more complicated than it really is. (See the sidebar on pp. 116-117 for how to mark the angled tenons on the first rail.)

Cutting the angled tenons Angled tenons are not significantly harder to cut than straight tenons. The same tenoning jig used for the straight tenons works equally well for angled ones (see the sidebar on p. 46). The only change from cutting straight tenons is the addition of the wedge to hold the workpiece at the proper angle. If you move the wedge up and down in the jig (you may have to cut off the tip), the side rail, which stays in the same position up

against the bottom of the tenoning template, will move out or in relative to the template. This will effectively change the tenon location, maybe even enough to avoid adjusting the tenoning template in or out.

Set up first for the front tenons. Attach the wedge firmly to the jig. Keep in mind that the outside faces of the side rails reference off the wedge for the front tenons, the inside faces for the rear tenons. This is what enables us to cut two different angles with the same wedge. Be sure to mark the tenon locations appropriately for the front or the rear. Cut the front tenons first. Reset the tenoning template (or move the wedge), and cut the rear tenons (see the photo at left). When these are done, lay out the tops and bottoms of the tenons, and cut them down to the layout lines. Round over the tops and bottoms of the tenons (see p. 111), and move on to testing and fitting the joints.

If you have a tenoning jig for a tablesaw, it is also easy to use the wedge to hold the workpiece at the correct angle for cutting the cheeks. The tablesaw requires numerous careful setups to cut the shoulders, however, including angling the blade. I have never had much success with cutting the shoulders accurately this way, although other woodworkers claim that it's easy enough after they've done it a lot. A flat-bottomed dado set works better because it cuts away all of the wood at once—the shoulders along with the cheeks. The problem here is that the tenoning jig must be very stable because you're cutting end grain—and a lot of

CUTTING TENONS WITHOUT ANGLES

Don't want to get involved with cutting angled tenons at all? There is a way around it that works well but wastes considerably more wood. For this, you will need to draw out a plan view of a side rail accurately on paper; draw the rail as if it were in place on a chair with the front and rear rails horizontal on the page (see the drawing below). Then draw a rectangle that completely contains the side rail and its tenons. You will need a piece of 12/4 stock as wide as this rectangle for each rail; it would be roughly 3⅞ in. for this chair. Locate the tenons where they need

to go by measuring. Cut straight tenons on both ends, but offset them from one another as determined by your drawing. Then cut the sides of the piece according to the layout (bandsaw, then clean up on the jointer or with a hand plane). I've seen some chairs where only the outside face of the rail was angled. I think this looks odd, but then again someone who crawls around on the floor looking at the undersides of chairs probably has a minimal grasp of what is actually odd.

CUTTING SIDE RAILS WITHOUT ANGLES

Step 1: Lay out the side rail.

Step 2: Cut the straight tenons offset from each other.

Step 3: Cut away the waste.

Step 4: Some furniture makers leave the inside uncut. This looks pretty weird to anyone looking under the chair.

it. Cut very slowly and carefully. Make sure you know where the blade will emerge on the back of the jig, and be sure that fingers, metal screws, or the jig itself are not in the path of the blade. There is also a tendency to split out the back edge of the workpiece, so be sure to back up the cut with a scrap board.

Cutting tenons with any method can get a little confusing. Since the side rails are mirror images of each other and the joints are different at the front and the rear of the chair, you have to make sure you are cutting the joints on the right end of the right pieces at the correct angle. The solution—both simple and effective—is to mark out your pieces carefully with letters, numbers, arrows, hieroglyphics, or whatever helps you know what you're doing at all times.

Once all of the tenons are cut, miter the inside corners of the front tenons, and check and adjust the fit of the joints, including the lengths of the tenons. Then dry-fit the basic framework together. It's starting to look like a chair at this point!

Correcting angle problems

What do you do if—despite your best efforts at checking your angles beforehand—the angle is still a little off? Fortunately, the solutions are not all that drastic.

Changing the length of the front rail is usually all that's necessary. If you have a gap between the side rail and the legs on the outside at the front and the inside at the rear, make the front rail shorter. Just recut the tenon with a new shoulder. Gaps on the inside at the front and the outside at the rear of the side rail mean you'll have to remake a slightly longer front rail. In either case, try to get a measurement for how much longer or shorter by dry-fitting the chair together without the front rail. Clamp up so that the joints are tight, but be very gentle with the clamps so you don't introduce distortion from the pressure. Even with a mea-

ACCOMMODATING A SLIP SEAT: PART 1

The upholstered seat on this chair rests on top of the rails. But there is another option that is a little more involved but more elegant— recessing the seat into a rabbet in the rails. This is the way a chair with a true slip seat is made. You should address this as you finish up the work on the rails because much of the work for this involves the rails. The rabbet for the seat should leave a lip that is ¼ in. wide on the top of the front and side rails and should be ¼ in. deep. Cut the rabbet on the tablesaw or with the router on the insides (check this twice to be sure) of the tops of the rails. That is all that needs to be done now. When the chair is together, you'll need to cut down an area on the tops of the front legs (see the sidebar on p. 128).

surement, it wouldn't be a bad idea to "sneak up" on the right length with small changes until the fit is just right.

MAKING THE SLATS

With the basic framework done, it's time to move on to the slats. Cut the stock for the slats out of 1-in.-thick flatsawn stock. I like the look of the quartered grain that results, and the slats will match reasonably well even if you can't get them all from the same board. (This is more of an issue when making a set of chairs.)

With the design of this chair, the slats (and therefore the tenons at the top of the slats) should be at right angles to the crest rail. The bottoms of the slats angle back from the rear rail. The best way to determine this angle is with a bevel gauge held against a straightedge running from the rear rail to the crest rail and aligned with the top of the rear rail. Then make a wedge that will cut tenons at this angle—again the master angle, which is the difference between the angle on the bevel gauge and 90 degrees.

Tenoning the slats

As a test, start the slat joinery by cutting the angled tenon on the bottom of an extra slat, trimmed so that it reaches to just below the crest rail. Inserted into the assembled chair back, this will show you quite precisely whether or not the angle is correct. In fact, it will show you too precisely. If the test slat is within $\frac{1}{16}$ in. of centered on the crest rail mortise, go ahead and cut the rest of

the angled tenons. The flexibility of the slats will still allow a good fit. If you're off more than that, adjust the angle, and test it again.

You can also get an accurate measurement of the length of the slats between tenons with this test piece by extending a ruler up from its end to the bottom of the crest rail. Mark the shoulder-to-shoulder lengths on the fronts—the longer sides—of the slats, then cut the right-angled tenons on the tops. There is a little room for error (of course, you should try not to take advantage of it, but it's nice to know it's there), but only if the slats are all the same length between shoulders. Since we previously cut the crest rail mortises long, there should be room to get the rail tenons in the mortises even if the distance between the crest rail and upper rail tenons is slightly off. If necessary, you can cut down the rail tenons a little more. Make sure everything fits now before proceeding to the glue-up.

PLANING, SCRAPING, AND SANDING

There are a lot of parts to plane, scrape, and sand. But most are small and quickly cleaned up. The critical areas are right around the mortises. Be careful not to angle or round over these areas or the tenons will not be able to seat tightly. With this firmly in mind, it is nice to ease the transitions into the side rail flats. This helps with the flow of the leg (even more important on a curved leg) but also gets rid of the ridge where the flat meets the rest of the leg.

ADDING OPTIONAL STRETCHERS

I'll state this right up front. Stretchers on a chair like this are a real challenge. Each one will need to be individually fit, and many of them will have compound angles at both ends. But they do add considerable strength and durability to a chair, and the process of fitting them, while slow and methodical, is quite satisfying.

Deciding on the stretcher locations and sizes is a design decision. There are many many different configurations and even more ways to implement these configurations. (See p. 7 for some of these possibilities.) I've chosen a simple-looking arrangement for this chair because it seems to fit in well with the overall design (see the drawing on p. 106 for the location of the stretchers). The stretchers are ¾ in. by 1 in.

The front and rear stretchers should be treated differently from the side stretchers. Ideally, the joinery for these should be cut along with the rest of the leg joinery, while the stock is still square. If you've cut the rear legs from the middle of a board, the rear stretcher mortises should be cut referencing off the side rail flats just like most of the other joints. The mortising block works well for this. When it comes time to taper the front and rear legs, the tapers should start below the stretchers. This way, the front and rear stretchers will have straight tenons and will be exactly the same length as the rails.

The side stretchers are different; they need to be marked and joined after the basic frame of the chair is cut and fit together. Even the layout is a little complicated. You can't just measure up from the bottoms of the legs because the legs are at different angles. So while the chair is still

The bevel square is handy for lots of things. Here it helps with the compound angle on the stretcher.

dry-assembled, make a simple pattern to mark the location. The pattern is really just a piece of ¼-in. plywood cut so that when it is held up to the chair legs, the stretcher locations (in this case, 10¼ in. to the top of the stretcher) are marked. Since the stretchers are parallel to the floor on this chair, the plywood is just ripped to a width equal to the stretcher height. If you want the stretchers to angle back, the plywood could be cut that way.

To cut the mortises, disassemble the chair, then transfer the mortise locations to the front of the back leg and the back of the front leg. Rout the mortises with the outside of the legs clamped against the mortising block. Then reassemble the chair.

Now comes the fun with angles. The angled wedge you used for cutting the side rail tenons gives you the side-to-side angle. But the up-and-down angle is different on the front and the back of the stretcher. I use the bevel square to determine this angle by holding the base against the leg and lining up the adjustable blade with the stretcher marks (see the photo on the facing page). Then transfer this angle to the face of the wedge. Use the tenoning jig with the wedge, and line up the stretcher with the angled line (see the photo at right). Now cut a test stretcher from some extra stock so that it just fits between the legs and into its mortise. Seat it tightly in the mortise, and check to see where the other side is aiming. If the stretcher is not aiming right at the mark on the other leg, adjust the angle and try again.

When you have the angle right, cut the actual joint on a stretcher. Then use the test stretcher again to measure the exact between-tenon length, and mark the shoulder location on the other end. The same process is necessary for the tenon on the other side of the stretcher (aiming at the back leg) and the rest of the joints. Remember that the joints on opposite sides of the chair will be mirror images of each other. You'll have to mark an angle the opposite way on the wedge.

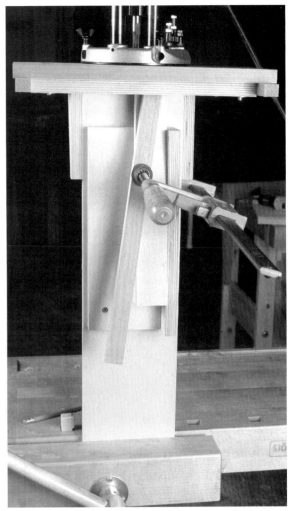

This setup is for cutting a compound-angled tenon with an angled wedge; the slat is aligned and clamped on an angled line drawn on the wedge.

ASSEMBLING THE CHAIR

The glue-up proceeds in stages, and each stage is easily manageable. Nevertheless, it does help to stay away from fast-setting glues. The first step is to assemble the slats with the rear and crest rails. Apply glue in the mortises and very sparingly on the tenons, then insert the slats into the rear rail mortises. The crest rail goes on top, starting at one end and working across, slat by slat. When all of the tenons are in their mortises, clamp up carefully. If you can clamp this up so that all of the joints are tight both front and back, then you need not go further for the moment. But it isn't easy to clamp effectively with the angled tenons. If your joints are not closing up, simply glue the rear legs on at the same time. Protect the side rail mortises in the legs with some filler blocks to prevent the clamps from crushing them, then clamp the legs on. Before you tight-

USING CAULS FOR THE GLUE-UP

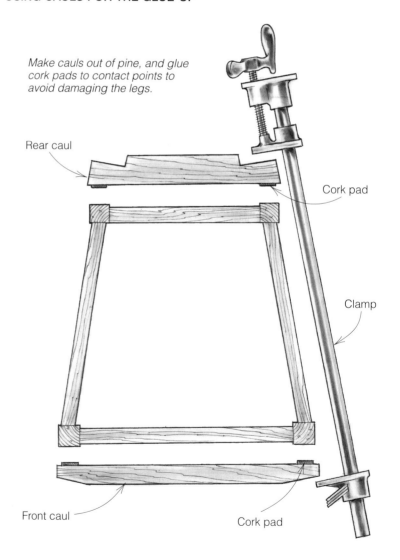

Make cauls out of pine, and glue cork pads to contact points to avoid damaging the legs.

Rear caul

Cork pad

Clamp

Front caul

Cork pad

en these clamps, clamp the slats tightly between the crest and rear rails. Tighten up the legs, and set the back assembly aside.

Glue the front legs onto the front rail next. Be sure to use the filler blocks in the side rail mortises here, too, and set the front leg assembly down with the side rail mortises facing up.

For the final glue-up, it helps to make up some simple cauls (see the draw-ing on the facing page). Clamp the cauls on the front and rear rails be-fore starting the actual glue-up (see the photo below). Then it's a simple matter to get side rail tenons into front and back mortises and put on the clamps. Clamp slowly and evenly until everything seats, then congrat-ulate yourself. You could throw a scrap piece of plywood down over the rails and have a seat, or just be ca-sual about it and wait until the chair is out of clamps.

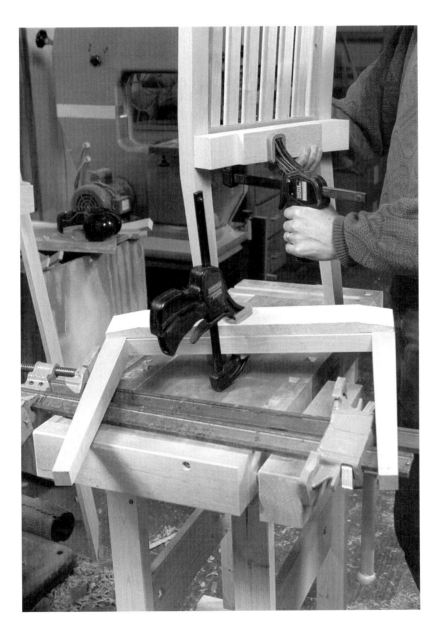

It helps to clamp the cauls to the front and rear assemblies prior to the final glue-up. This way you don't have to struggle with hold-ing them in place while you're trying to do everything else.

Here I'm using a straightedge and bevel gauge to determine the obtuse angle for the front corner blocks.

THE FINISHING TOUCHES

Now is the time to apply a finish (see the appendix on p. 195). In between coats, you can work on corner blocks, the seat blank, and glides.

Cutting and fitting corner blocks

On this chair, which has a trapezoidal seat, the front and rear corner blocks are different (see the Top view in the drawing on p. 106). To determine the angles, start by marking off equal lengths from the corners (about 6 in.—this is not where the blocks will go, it's just easier to get a good angle this way) on one side of the front rail and an adjoining side rail. Lay a straightedge from mark to mark, and set your bevel gauge to the obtuse angle formed by the straightedge and a rail to the outside of the triangle (see the photo above). Angle the tablesaw blade to match this angle, and crosscut the corner blocks to about 5½ in. long. Thanks to the laws of geometry, once the correct angle is set for the front blocks, you shouldn't have to change it for the rear. But you will need to cut the rear blocks differently—upright on the tablesaw. To do this safely, you need a jig that will ride on the rip fence and has a fence to hold the blocks perpendicular to the tablesaw (see the drawing on the facing page). Though simple, corner blocks need to fit well, so test out the fit carefully. If you need to

A JIG FOR CUTTING REAR CORNER BLOCKS

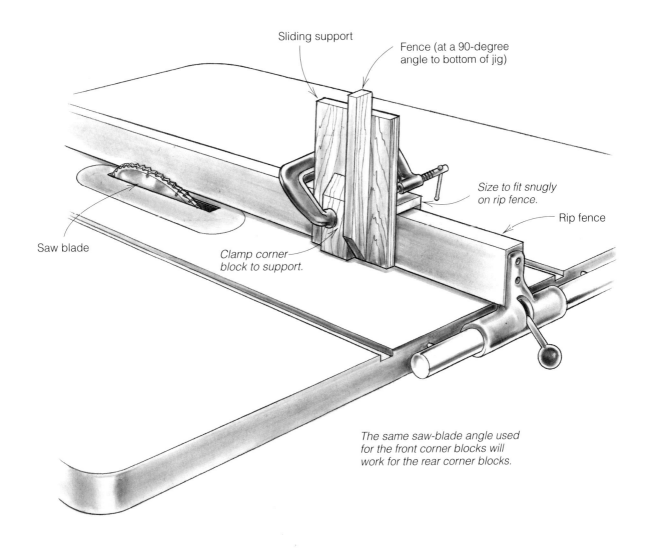

Sliding support

Fence (at a 90-degree angle to bottom of jig)

Size to fit snugly on rip fence.

Rip fence

Saw blade

Clamp corner block to support.

The same saw-blade angle used for the front corner blocks will work for the rear corner blocks.

ACCOMMODATING A SLIP SEAT: PART 2

The router pattern is clamped into place in preparation for finishing the slip seat recess. I'm using a flush-trimming bit with the bearing on top.

If you've opted to make the chair with a real slip seat recessed down into the rails, you now have to finish the job by routing the top of the front legs so that the recess is complete. This can be done with a router and a pattern or with a router wasting away the bulk of the wood, making the final cuts by hand with a chisel and a gouge. The upholstered seat can't fill a sharp corner, and the corner would look wrong, especially filled with dirt and crumbs. So the goal here is to make a smoothly radiused inside corner. (A ⅜-in. radius is about right.)

To make a pattern, draw one of the front corners of the chair by tracing the outside of the rails and one leg onto a piece of ¾-in. plywood. Next draw a line ¼ in. to the inside of the traced rail line to locate the lip. As the side rail comes forward into the corner, make a smooth transition to parallel to the side of the leg and then around to the front rail. Now cut out the inside of the pattern, and smooth. To use the pattern, clamp it to the front and side rails of the chair so the edges are just flush with the inside of the rabbeted edge of the rails (see the photo above). Rout away the waste on the top of the leg with an overhead-bearing flush-trimming bit (often referred to as a pattern maker's bit). Set the depth of cut to just touch the bottom of the rabbet. Then flip the pattern over, and rout the other corner.

To size the seat blank, you'll need to trace the shape of the outside of the seat, then draw lines the appropriate amount to the inside so the seat blank will fit into the recess. Cut out the blank (or just a pattern to start), and test out the fit. Try to leave a ³⁄₃₂-in. space on all sides to allow room for the fabric and batting. When you have the seat upholstered, you should ask for a single welt (a bit of cording covered in the same fabric) to be stapled to the underside of the seat blank around the front and sides. This will fill in any gaps between the seat and the recess and is a nice detail (see the photo below).

The slip seat rests neatly on the recess. Note the welt, which is stapled to the bottom edge of the seat.

make adjustments, don't bother to correct both sides—just recut one angle. Now drill pilot holes for the screws that will attach the corner blocks by placing one block at a time bevel down on the drill press table. Clamp it to a fence clamped down to the table, then drill two holes on each side with a drill bit and countersink.

Making a seat blank

Lay a piece of $\frac{3}{8}$-in. or $\frac{1}{2}$-in. plywood at least $16\frac{5}{8}$ in. by 20 in. on your seat. Mark the location of the rear legs on the back edge of the plywood, then cut two notches for the legs, $\frac{1}{8}$ in. deep and $\frac{1}{8}$ in. to the inside of the legs. Now position the plywood with the back edge just touching the rear rail and centered on the rear legs, and trace around the outside of the front and side rails from below. Modify the front corners of the seat to get rid of the bulges for the legs. Cut out the blank, smooth all of the edges, and ease the corners a little.

Now place the cut-out seat blank on the chair frame. Try flipping it over. Is the chair symmetrical? With the seat blank in position, trace the corner block locations onto the bottom of the blank. Remove the blank, and drill four $\frac{7}{32}$-in. holes through it, centered on the corner blocks (as traced). Reposition the seat blank on the chair, and drill down through the corner blocks. Pound 8-32 T-nuts into the holes in the top of the blank, and counterbore the underside of the corner blocks for 8-32 by 2-in. or $2\frac{1}{2}$-in. machine screws and washers.

As I mentioned in Chapter 4, I send my seat blanks out to be upholstered. I'd much rather have some-one who is good at it do the work. I usually get 1-in. foam and one layer of batting, and I ask for a rather flat look. You will need about $\frac{3}{4}$ yard of fabric, but this will cover two seats. If you want to attempt the upholstery yourself, see the sidebar on p. 84, which tells you how.

Attach the upholstered seat with the machine screws and washers.

Attaching glides

Glides are important on this chair. The rear legs angle back and are likely to have some short grain across the back corners. The glides will help protect those corners, all of the bottom edges, and the floor. Turn the chair over on a padded table, and hammer the glides into the bottom of the legs.

On the slat-back chair, we've done a lot with the idea of cutting joinery in square parts before adding shapes or angles. This is a very useful method, both in practice and in concept. We've also seen that, with the right approach, angled tenons are not really harder to make than straight tenons—a major step forward in developing your skills in chairmaking.

7

NEOCLASSICAL CHAIR

With this chair, we start to incorporate a little more style. The neoclassical chair is not entirely different from what we've seen before, however. Note the similar side frame construction between this chair and the dowel chair in Chapter 3. The side frames on the neoclassical chair are more refined; they are mortised and tenoned together and have much more shaping. But both are simple, flat structures that are then joined together to make the chair. From a chairmaking point of view, one of the more significant features of the neoclassical chair is the curved horizontal back slat—something we have not encountered yet (see the drawing on p. 132 for dimensions on all parts).

The style of the neoclassical chair derives from the early nineteenth century idea of the ancient Greek klismos chair and is most commonly associated with Duncan Phyfe, the most successful cabinetmaker working in this style (see the photo on p. 24). This type of chair is a clear case of visual design taking precedent over sound structural design. Front and rear rails on most chairs of this style were much narrower than on this version, leaving little room for effective joinery. (Twin tenons were common, and corner blocks helped.) The intricate back structures were elegant but fragile. And legs shaped like these (called sabre legs) have inherent problems with short grain.

MAKING THE SIDE FRAMES

Start work on the side frames by drawing up a full-size pattern of a complete side on a piece of ¼-in. plywood (see the drawing on p. 133). Before cutting the pattern, examine it carefully to be sure the lines flow. Look at the curves from a low angle—this will help you spot the places that need more work. Then cut out the pattern, and smooth it carefully. Keep sighting down the curves to be sure they remain smooth and flowing (see the photo on p. 134). Making up the pattern as a whole helps ensure that the lines will be pleasing.

Front view

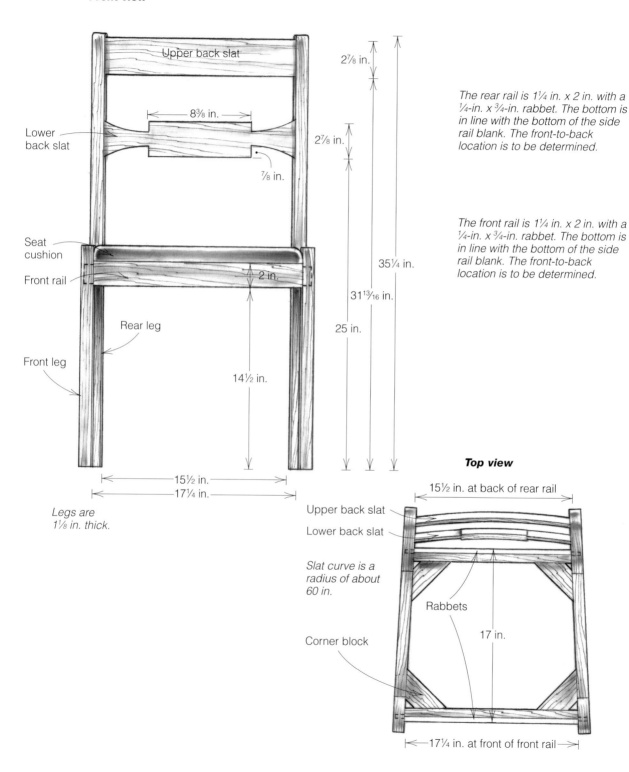

Upper back slat

8⅜ in.

Lower
back slat

⅞ in.

2⅞ in.

2⅞ in.

Seat
cushion

Front rail

2 in.

Rear leg

35¼ in.

31¹³⁄₁₆ in.

25 in.

Front leg

14½ in.

15½ in.
17¼ in.

*Legs are
1⅛ in. thick.*

*The rear rail is 1¼ in. x 2 in. with a
¼-in. x ¾-in. rabbet. The bottom is
in line with the bottom of the side
rail blank. The front-to-back
location is to be determined.*

*The front rail is 1¼ in. x 2 in. with a
¼-in. x ¾-in. rabbet. The bottom is
in line with the bottom of the side
rail blank. The front-to-back
location is to be determined.*

Top view

15½ in. at back of rear rail

Upper back slat

Lower back slat

*Slat curve is a
radius of about
60 in.*

Rabbets

17 in.

Corner block

17¼ in. at front of front rail

PATTERN FOR SIDE FRAMES

Scale: 1 square = 1 in.

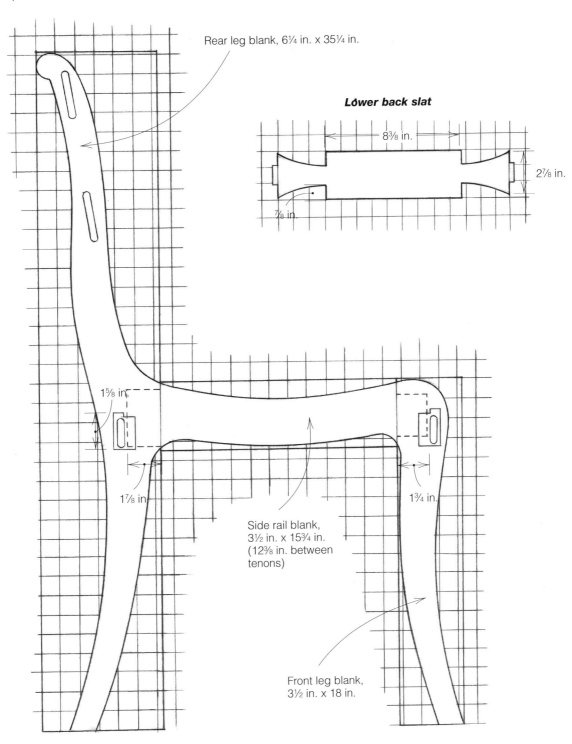

Rear leg blank, 6¼ in. x 35¼ in.

Lower back slat

8⅜ in.

2⅞ in.

⅞ in.

1⅝ in.

1⅞ in.

1¾ in.

Side rail blank,
3½ in. x 15¾ in.
(12⅜ in. between
tenons)

Front leg blank,
3½ in. x 18 in.

Sighting down a curve makes it easy to see any uneven places on it. Here I'm marking an uneven spot.

straight up-and-down grain. Avoid grain that curves opposite to the curve of the leg. If you can't avoid these problems when laying out rectangular blanks, you should cut the legs to shape before cutting the joinery. This will give you more control over how you utilize the grain.

Also try to avoid woods that are hard to plane or that are difficult to work in general. I opted for mahogany because it planes and sands beautifully. Walnut would be another good choice. These woods are also in keeping with the style of the chair.

Cutting the joints first

Cutting rectangular blanks for the legs and side rails simplifies the joinery and the layout. Cut the blanks to the sizes shown in the drawing on p. 133, then mark out and cut the mortises and tenons. For the side rail joints on this chair, I recommend ¹/₂-in. mortises and tenons (see the drawing on the facing page). This will require a new tenoning template for the tenoning jig, with a ³/₈-in. strip down the middle and a wider opening (see p. 46 for details on constructing the tenoning jig and template). Once the side rail mortises and tenons are cut, dry-fit and clamp the parts together, then trace the chair pattern onto the dry-fit side frames. While the parts are still together, lay out the front and rear rail mortises (see the drawing on p. 133). Pull the side frames apart, and rout the rail mortises with the plunge router and fence (see the photo on the facing page).

Routing the back slat mortises

Routing the back slat mortises requires a different approach because they are not quite in line and are at slightly different angles. Template mortising is perfect for this, and you

You can proceed either by milling your chosen wood into rectangular blanks and cutting joinery before cutting to shape (as with the dowel chair), or you can cut out the shapes you need, establish the necessary side rail flats, and then cut the joinery. Cutting rectangular blanks first wastes more wood, but your decision should be based on more than just the quantity of wood wasted. Take time to examine the wood carefully. You don't want the problems inherent in the shape of the legs worsened by having the grain run across the leg. On the front leg, the grain should ideally run on a curve with the curve of the leg or in a line from top to bottom. On the rear leg, try to find grain that curves with the overall shape of the leg, or go with

LAYOUT FOR SIDE RAIL MORTISES AND TENONS

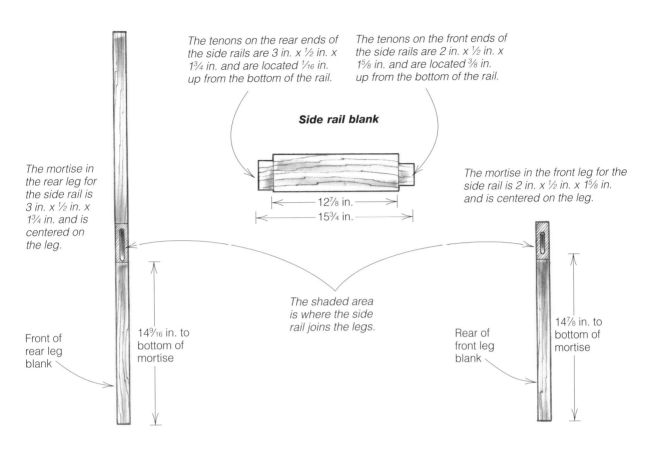

The tenons on the rear ends of the side rails are 3 in. x ½ in. x 1¾ in. and are located 1/16 in. up from the bottom of the rail.

The tenons on the front ends of the side rails are 2 in. x ½ in. x 1⅝ in. and are located ⅜ in. up from the bottom of the rail.

Side rail blank

12⅞ in.

15¾ in.

The mortise in the rear leg for the side rail is 3 in. x ½ in. x 1¾ in. and is centered on the leg.

The mortise in the front leg for the side rail is 2 in. x ½ in. x 1⅝ in. and is centered on the leg.

The shaded area is where the side rail joins the legs.

Front of rear leg blank

14 9/16 in. to bottom of mortise

Rear of front leg blank

14⅞ in. to bottom of mortise

Use a fence or edge guide to carefully rout the rear rail mortise on the still uncut leg blank.

THE SLAT-MORTISING TEMPLATE

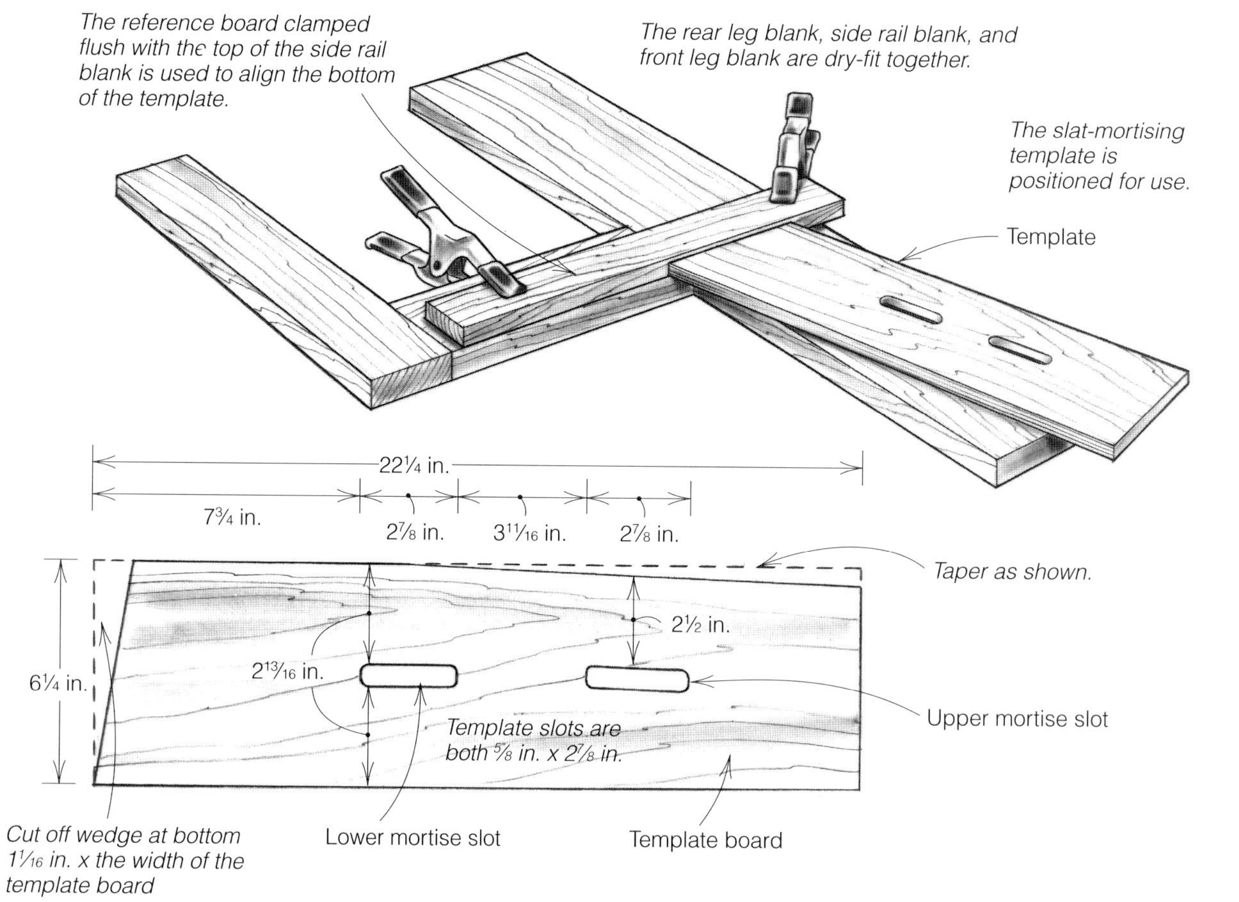

The reference board clamped flush with the top of the side rail blank is used to align the bottom of the template.
The rear leg blank, side rail blank, and front leg blank are dry-fit together.
The slat-mortising template is positioned for use.
Template
22 1/4 in.
7 3/4 in.
2 7/8 in.
3 11/16 in.
2 7/8 in.
Taper as shown.
6 1/4 in.
2 13/16 in.
2 1/2 in.
Upper mortise slot
Template slots are both 5/8 in. x 2 7/8 in.
Cut off wedge at bottom 1 1/16 in. x the width of the template board
Lower mortise slot
Template board

can also take advantage of the fact that the parts are still rectangular. You should lay out both mortises on a single template to simplify the process and to keep precise alignment between the slats.

To make the slat-mortising template, cut a piece of 3/8-in. (or thicker) plywood 6 1/4 in. wide and 22 1/4 in. long. Lay out the lower mortise slot according to the drawing above. With the router's fence attached, plunge-rout a 1/2-in. slot along one side of the intended opening, then adjust the fence to widen the slot to 5/8 in.

Now taper the side of the template (I bandsawed and sanded straight and smooth), and locate and rout the upper mortise slot as you did the lower, but with the fence riding on the angled edge. Finally, angle the bottom of the template, as indicated in the drawing.

How did I arrive at this? This unusual-looking template arrangement is the direct result of playing around with the slat locations on a mock-up of the chair (see the photo on the facing page). I kept trying different locations until I had something that was reasonably comfortable and in proportion with the rest of the chair. Once I had the slat locations on the mock-up, I had to figure out a way to

Mock-ups should be made with scraps you have on hand. I fooled around with this one until it was quite comfortable (for me, at least).

get those results reliably on a finished piece. A little work with a ruler and bevel gauge led to the slat-mortising template as described.

To cut the mortises, first clamp the legs and side rail assembly together so that the joints seat tightly. Then, clamp a reference board flush with the top of the side rail, and place the angled bottom end of the tenoning template against it. Adjust the template side to side until the mortises are located roughly in the center of the actual leg. It's hard to see anything with the template in place, so trace the openings, then remove the template to check their location. Reposition, if necessary, and clamp in place (see the drawing on the facing page). Set the depth of cut to give a ⅞-in.-deep mortise, and rout. For the other side of the chair, the procedure is the same. Flip the template over, and use measurements

ROUTING MORTISES STRAIGHT UP AND DOWN

You could also rout the mortises in line with the edge of the rectangular blanks. This has some advantages: It is easier to rout the mortises, and it avoids compound-angled tenons on the back slats. But neither of these are big problems, and if you don't cut compound angles in the slats, you have to bandsaw the slats at an angle to compensate (see the drawing below). The joint size is limited to ¼ in. by 1¾ in. with this method, so it is slightly weaker.

AN ALTERNATE METHOD OF CUTTING BACK SLAT MORTISES

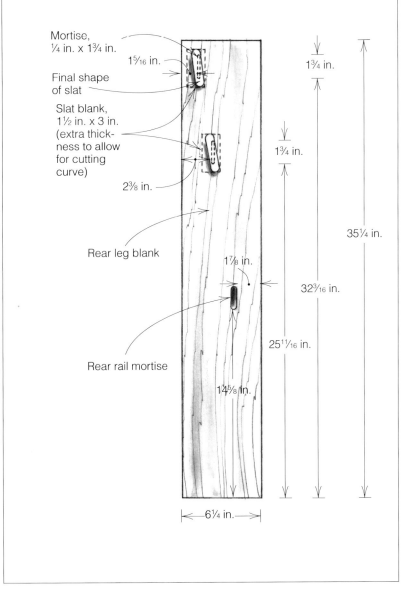

Mortise, ¼ in. x 1¾ in.

1⁵⁄₁₆ in.

Final shape of slat

Slat blank, 1½ in. x 3 in. (extra thickness to allow for cutting curve)

2⅜ in.

Rear leg blank

1⅞ in.

Rear rail mortise

14⅝ in.

1¾ in.

1¾ in.

35¼ in.

32³⁄₁₆ in.

25¹¹⁄₁₆ in.

6¼ in.

Set up the shooting board to cut the side rail flat perpendicular to the bottom of the chair.

Hand-plane the side rail flat with the rear leg clamped to the shooting board.

from the already routed side as a reference to locate the template in the same place.

Now disassemble the chair parts, and cut to shape. Smooth out the curves, but don't worry about the transition curves from the legs into the side rails other than to avoid damaging the fragile points on the side rails. The transitions can be sanded once the sides are glued up. Note that the waste from the back legs can be used for the front and rear rails.

Cutting the parts first

If you don't have enough wood— cutting the rear legs out of rectangular blanks *is* wasteful—or if the grain doesn't allow you to cut the joinery first, you'll have to cut the rear legs to shape, and then cut the joinery (similar to what was done in Chapter 6). You could cut the front legs the same way, but the savings are minimal for all the extra work. First, mark the chair pattern for the side rail flats location. The mark doesn't have to be precise because you'll be trimming the flats later—just be sure that you leave enough wood. Then trace the pattern onto the wood, paying particular attention to the grain, and cut out the legs.

To trim the flats, use a shooting board (see the drawing on p. 110). You will need to locate and draw out the leg shape on the side of the shooting board accurately to align the side rail flat correctly. Tack a straight reference board across the bottoms of the legs on the pattern, and using a square, locate and trace the pattern on the face of the shooting board so that the flat is perpendicular to the reference board and, ultimately, to the floor (see the top photo). The angle of the side rail flat is more important than its actual location, which should be roughly in

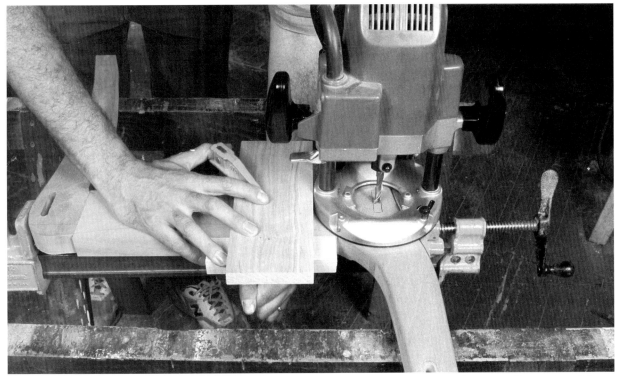

Rout the rear rail mortise with the legs already shaped. The fence is under the author's right hand; the cleat for the fence sits on the still-straight side rail.

the center of the transition curve from the back to the seat rail. (Both legs must be the same, however.) A hand plane works well to trim the flats (see the bottom photo on the facing page), but you could also use a router if you place a board on top of the shooting board, then set the router bit to cut flush with the top of the jig.

Cutting mortises and tenons for the side rails Lay out and rout the side rail mortises while the legs are still clamped to the shooting board (see the drawing on p. 135 for the specifications), using the shooting board just like a mortising block. To calculate the length of the side rail between tenons, lay the legs in position on the $\frac{1}{4}$-in. plywood pattern and measure. Add the tenon lengths (mortise depths less $\frac{1}{32}$ in.) to get the overall length, cut the rail as a rectangular blank, and tenon it. (For more on cutting the $\frac{1}{2}$-in. tenons, see p. 134.) Then dry-

assemble the chair side, and mark out the shape of the side rail, but don't cut it to shape yet.

Mortising for the other rails and the slats For the front and rear rail mortises, you'll need to make up a very simple mortising jig: a cleat to reference off the side rail and a fence perpendicular to the cleat for the router to ride against. First, clamp the legs and side rails together. (Be sure to use clamp pads.) Mark out the mortise locations carefully (see the drawing on p. 133), then line up the cleat to position the router with a $\frac{3}{8}$-in. bit, and clamp (see the photo above). Set the depth of cut to $\frac{7}{8}$ in., and rout the mortises to the marked-out lines.

The procedure for mortising for back slats is the same as described in "Routing the back slat mortises" on p. 134. Even though the legs are already cut to shape, the side rails

Since the grain direction in this corner makes it difficult to carve, you'll need to file the corner of the scroll.

should still be straight. Make sure the side frames are clamped together for this.

Once all of the mortises are cut, disassemble the side frames, cut the side rails to shape, and smooth all of the parts. Be careful of the fragile corners of the side rails, and wait to sand the transition curves until the side frame is glued together.

Gluing the side frames together
For gluing up the side frames, you'll need to make cauls so you can clamp the legs easily. Cutoffs from cutting the legs to shape will work, or just use the legs or the pattern to mark out the appropriate shapes on some scrap wood. Sand the cauls smooth, and apply cork pads to the inner faces of the cauls, so you don't mar the legs. (This is particularly necessary when working with softer woods.) Then spread glue in the mortises and lightly on the tenons, and clamp the side frames together.

Smoothing the shaped edges
Now finish smoothing all of the edges. Drum sanders in a few different sizes work well on the transition curves, but be sure to hand-sand afterward because the sanding drums usually leave a distinctly different surface. Profile the edges with a ¼-in. roundover bit, then carve the scroll detail with a chisel and a file (see the photo above). The grain runs the wrong way to use a chisel on both sides of the corner.

CUTTING AND TENONING THE RAILS
The challenge in cutting and tenoning the front and rear rails is determining the correct angle and position for the tenons. This is easily done with a full-size drawing, as shown in the drawings on the facing page. (The positioning jig from Chapter 6 doesn't work with this chair because the side frames are already together.)

Draw a rectangle 17¼ in. wide and 17 in. high, and at the bottom (the back of the chair), measure in ⅞ in. from both sides to create the necessary trapezoid shape. You can control the distance between rails by where you locate the rail tenons. Adjust the tenon locations so the rails will be 17 in. apart (outside edge to outside edge). To calculate this, first dry-fit the legs and side rail. Subtract the distance between the outside of the rail mortises from 17 in. and divide by 2 (see the drawings at right). The result—the setback for each tenon— should be roughly ⅛ in.

Unfortunately, when you use the tenoning jig to cut the tenons, the front of the rail blank is hidden, so for the front rail, you need to transfer the shoulder lines around to the back. Use a bevel gauge (set to the actual shoulder angle, not the master angle) to transfer the lines around. Make sure the backs of your rails are narrower than the fronts.

There is a little more layout work on both rails before you cut. The tenon locations—set in roughly ⅛ in. at the shoulder line (the exact measurement should have been calculated above)—need to be transferred up to the end of the blank so you can set up to cut properly. The easiest way to do this is to mark the tenon location on the penciled shoulder line, cut the end of the blank to the shoulder angle, and use a square on the end of the blank to draw the line up from the shoulder (see the top drawing on p. 142 and the sidebar on p. 116 for more).

Once you've determined the master angle (and cut a wedge), the rail lengths, and the tenon positions, size the actual rail stock, and cut the ⅜-in. tenons. Pay particular attention to what you're cutting where—the tenons should be toward the front of the front rail and toward the back of the rear rail. Both front rail tenons will use the same setup, while both rear tenons will use a different setup. Trim and round over the ends of the tenons, then fit them to the mortises.

Rabbet the tops of the front and rear rails ¼ in. deep and ⅝ in. wide for the seat. Then chamfer the edges with a plane or router. Dry-assemble the chair frame together, and clamp tight in preparation for calculating the back slat lengths.

CALCULATING RAIL LENGTHS, ANGLES, AND DISTANCE APART

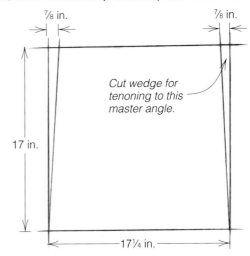

⅞ in. ⅞ in.

Cut wedge for tenoning to this master angle.

17 in.

17¼ in.

Top view

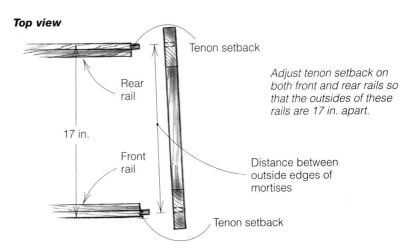

Tenon setback

Rear rail

17 in.

Front rail

Tenon setback

Adjust tenon setback on both front and rear rails so that the outsides of these rails are 17 in. apart.

Distance between outside edges of mortises

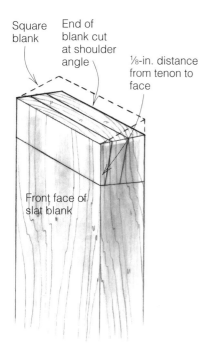

Square blank

End of blank cut at shoulder angle

⅛-in. distance from tenon to face

Front face of slat blank

MAKING THE BACK SLATS

The curved back slats are cut to shape from rectangular blanks 2⅞ in. by 1¼ in. by roughly 17 in. after the tenons have been cut. Unfortunately, the length is not the same as the rear rail because the side frames are not parallel and the slats are located further back than the rear rail. The two slats will each be different lengths and will have a slight compound angle.

To measure for the back slats, mark lines ⅛ in. in front of the slat mortises (to locate the fronts of the slats), and measure from one side to the other ⅛ in. down from the mortises. This gives the widest measurement for each slat (from long point to long point). I used two rulers to get this inside measurement (see the top photo on the facing page). Center

these dimensions on the front of the slat blanks; these are the tenon shoulder lines. See the sidebar below to help you determine how to orient the grain on the front of your slat blanks.

As with the rail tenons, you need to transfer your marks to the back of the slat blanks, and figure out where to cut the tenons by transferring the intended setback of ⅛ in. up from the shoulder to the end of the blank (see the drawing at left). Make sure you know where the long points should be (on the lower front corners), but don't worry about marking the secondary angle precisely. The same wedge used to cut the rail tenons works as the primary wedge for the back slats. I calculated the angle of the secondary wedge by cutting a test slat, and measuring (and guessing) to see what was needed to

CHOOSING GRAIN DIRECTION ON THE SLATS

You can orient the grain a few different ways on these slats, and each way yields a different result. With quartersawn wood, the grain on a concave-shaped slat would be straight (if the grain really runs straight across; it didn't on my quartersawn slat in the photo at right). Flatsawn grain yields a concentric ring pattern. Diagonally angled grain (as seen on the end grain) shows a gentle arching when cut. Think about what you want. My preference is for the arching grain that comes from end grain that angles up to the top back corner. Whatever your choice, mark the orientation of the blanks.

Orientation of the growth rings on the back slats affects the grain pattern. From the top, we see quartersawn with a straight grain pattern, flatsawn with concentric ovals, and diagonally angled grain with an arched grain pattern.

fill the angled gap. Enlarging the taper to a workable size, I came up with a taper of ⅛ in. over 16 in. (It is easier to make an actual wedge measuring ¼ in. to ⅜ in. over 16 in.)

To set up the tenoning jig to cut the tenons in the blanks, start by installing the primary angle wedge. Tack the secondary wedge against the vertical fence (see the drawing in the sidebar below). Then clamp the already-marked slat blank into place. Center the tenoning template bar between the tenon marks on the end of the slat blank. Then, because you didn't lay out the secondary angle, set the depth of cut to the lowest point on the transferred shoulder line. (The actual long point is on the side of the slat facing the jig.)

Use two rulers to measure between the legs to size the back slat.

CUTTING COMPOUND-ANGLED TENONS

Cutting compound-angled tenons is really no more difficult than cutting any other tenon. The only real change is the addition of a secondary wedge (or an angled line, as we saw on p. 116). The tenoning jig is set up with one primary wedge for a simple angle, and the secondary wedge angles the workpiece from the fence. The secondary wedge is normally flipped over to cut the compound angle on the opposite side of a part (see the drawing at right). What *is* hard with compound angles is keeping track of exactly what angle has to be cut where. I usually mark the workpiece with exaggerated angles as a reminder so that I don't get confused when setting up to make the cut. It is also very important to keep track of where you should measure from to get the appropriate between-tenon length for a part. I try to make all of these measurements for compound-angled tenons from the longest point.

CUTTING COMPOUND-ANGLED TENONS

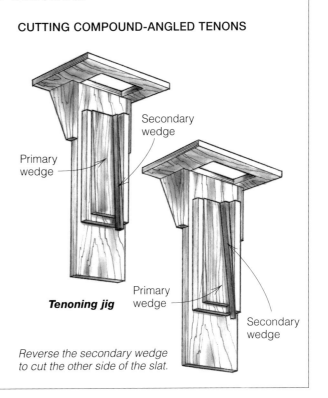

Tenoning jig

Secondary wedge

Primary wedge

Primary wedge

Secondary wedge

Reverse the secondary wedge to cut the other side of the slat.

DRAWING CURVES

There are many ways to draw smooth even curves. Here are two simple methods. You can make a large compass with a strip of wood, a nail, and a pencil. Drill two holes in the strip–the distance between the holes is the radius of the circle or arc. You can also take a thin strip of wood and spring it to a pleasing curve with a clamp (see the photo below). This doesn't necessarily give you the arc of a circle, but that doesn't usually matter.

Drawing a curve for a pattern is easy with a thin strip of wood bowed with a clamp. The exact parameters of the curve are hard to control, but as they say in boatbuilding, if it looks fair, it is fair.

Cut the tenons on a pair of test blanks first, and try them in the chair, using clamps to be sure the rail joints are tight. Adjust for any problems, and cut another test blank or recut as necessary. Once you have the right lengths and angles, mark out and cut the actual slat tenons, trim the tenons to size, and round them over.

Make up a pattern for the curve of the slats by drawing the arcs (see the sidebar above). Note that the back curve has a radius ⅝ in. larger than the front. Cut out and smooth the pattern, then mark out the curves on the slats. Cut them on the bandsaw.

Smoothing the slats is best done when they are clamped between bench dogs. When working on the front (the concave side) of the slat, use the cutoff from bandsawing the back to support the work. Round the edges with a ¼-in. roundover bit.

Now cut the lower slat to shape, using the same cutoff used for support while bandsawing. Smooth the sides with files and sandpaper, and clean up the inside corner with a chisel. Ease the edges slightly with sandpaper—this is not a full roundover.

ASSEMBLING THE CHAIR

The final glue-up for this chair is easy compared with most of the others in this book. Assemble everything you'll need first: four 2-ft. clamps with pads, glue, and a glue-spreading stick custom-made for the occasion. Spread glue in the mortises on one side of the chair and lightly on the matching tenons. Insert the tenons. Then spread glue in the mortises on the opposite side and lightly on the tenons, and insert the tenons one at a time in their mortises. Stand the chair up, and clamp.

THE FINISHING TOUCHES

As soon as you take the chair out of clamps, turn it over on a well-padded surface and hammer in some glides. This will help prevent damage to the fragile outside corners of the legs. Then move on to the final steps of completing the chair.

Applying a finish

I finished the chair with my usual oil and wax finish, as described in the appendix on p. 195. A chair like this would also look good with a dark mahogany stain or dye, followed by an oil and wax (or other) finish. If you do apply a stain first, simply wipe on each of the three coats of oil. (Sanding in each coat of oil would sand off color.)

Before staining, be sure to sand the unfinished chair all the way up to 400 grit. Then wipe the chair down with a damp rag to raise the grain, and resand carefully after it dries. After the last coat of oil has dried, wax the chair lightly (using 0000 steel wool to apply it), and buff with a soft cloth.

Adding corner blocks

It's difficult to determine the angle for cutting the front corner blocks by measuring right off the chair as we did in Chapter 6 because the side rails are neither flat on top nor on the same level as the front rail. Instead, use the bevel gauge to transfer the front angle to a piece of 1/4-in. plywood. Then, measuring from the point where the transferred line meets the edge, mark off points at equal distances on the edge and the angled line, and connect the points. Reset the bevel gauge to the acute angle between the edge and the line you just drew, and set the miter fence to this angle.

Cut the front blocks, and check to be sure they fit. Then cut the rear blocks, proceeding as for the front. Check the fit, then drill the countersunk pilot holes for the screws (at least four per block arranged in a line), and attach the corner blocks level with the rabbets in the front and rear rails. To get them level,

clamp a board across the rabbets to help align the blocks before attaching (see the photo at right). It's easiest to do this with the chair inverted on a padded surface.

Adding the seat blank

To determine the size of the seat blank, measure the inside of the chair frame, and then figure to leave roughly 3/32 in. all around for the fabric (the actual gap size depends on the thickness of the fabric you're planning to use). Cut the plywood to size, and check the fit. Ease the edges.

Place the seat blank in position, and trace the corner block locations onto the bottom of the blank. Remove the blank, then drill four 7/32-in. holes through it, centered on the corner blocks (as traced). Reposition the seat blank on the chair, and drill down through the corner blocks. Pound 8-32 T-nuts into the holes in the top of the blank, and counterbore the underside of the corner blocks for bolts and washers. You can either send the seat out to be upholstered, or upholster it yourself (see the sidebar on p. 84).

Attach the seat. Sit down, and contemplate your increasing mastery of the shapes and angles of chairmaking.

To install the corner blocks flush with the rabbets in the rails, I've clamped a scrap board from the front rail rabbet across to the back. Hold the corner block in place on the scrap board, and screw into position.

8

CAFÉ CHAIR

Pay attention to the chairs you see in restaurants and cafés, and you'll notice a lot of chairs like this one. What I like about this café chair is the interaction of all of the curves. This is exactly what makes the chair look so challenging to build. But the principles discussed earlier in the book still apply. Much of the joinery is cut when the boards are still rectangular (or with jigs that create the same effect). And even though it's hard to see where to establish reference surfaces on the curves, we can still create them.

The chair is constructed in two separate phases: the front legs with the front and U-shaped rails, and the rear legs with the horizontal slats. Both phases have elements that should be quite familiar by now, but both also cover some new ground.

MAKING THE FRONT ASSEMBLY

Most of the work in the front assembly goes into making the laminated U-shaped rail. But we start with the front legs, which are simple and straightforward.

Making the front legs

Cut the two front leg blanks to size, and lay out and rout the rail mortises (see the drawing on p. 148). Then taper the two inside faces of each leg. This is a gently curved taper, which I cut on the bandsaw. There are two ways to approach this. If you make a flexible pattern, you can mark out the second cut on the curved face

that results from the first cut. Or you can mark both faces on the blank, and cut the first face, stopping about 1/4 in. before the end of the cut. Shut down the saw, and back out of the cut. The waste piece with the marks for the second face on it will be held in place by the little uncut section. Cut the second face, then cut away the last 1/4 in. on the first face. Smooth the legs, taking care not to angle or round over the areas of the leg around the mortises where the rails seat.

Bending the U-shaped rail

The U-shaped rail is laminated from thin layers of wood. For the laminated rail, you will need enough veneer to make up a rail that is 1 in. thick, 2¾ in. to 3 in. wide (this is allowing for waste because the actual rail will only be 2½ in. wide), and about

CAFÉ CHAIR
Front view

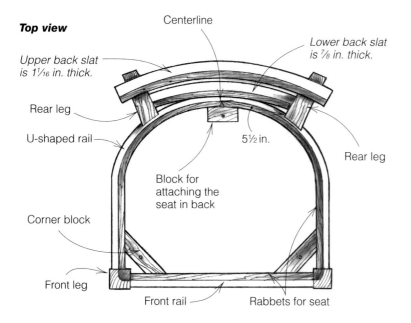

Upper back slat

3¼ in.

Lower back slat

2½ in.

Front leg

1½ in.

35¼ in.

Front rail

2½ in.

25 in.

17 in.

Rear legs

Front leg

¾ in.

1⅛ in.

Top view

Centerline

Upper back slat
is 1¹/₁₆ in. thick.

Lower back slat
is ⅞ in. thick.

Rear leg

U-shaped rail

5½ in.

Rear leg

Block for
attaching the
seat in back

Corner block

Front leg

Front rail

Rabbets for seat

48 in. long. I used ¹/₁₀ in. thick veneer for my chair. You may have to hunt around for this, but try to find the thickest veneer possible. It is also possible to saw your own—ripping thin strips to the outside of the blade on the tablesaw—but it takes a powerful saw and a big blade to do it. Ripping on the bandsaw works well, but it is best to plane the sawn surface, and this can occasionally destroy the veneer. Piecing the apron together out of solid stock is also a possibility, but the result is not quite as strong. The seams can be easily hidden by the rear legs, however.

There are two other important elements in a successful lamination. The first is the clamping method. Lamination requires a lot of pressure. For this chair, there isn't really room around the form for more than five or six clamps. But they should be high-quality bar clamps (½-in. pipe clamps don't exert enough pressure where it is needed). A vacuum press is another standard way to glue up laminations, but I find it rather challenging on this project.

Second is the choice of glue. Not all glues are appropriate for lamination. Most white and yellow woodworking glues will "creep" a little (that is, they slip a little under the constant tension of the wood trying to straighten out), which will affect the shape and, ultimately, the integrity of the U-shaped rail. There are a number of glues designed specifically for lamination. Of these, I use plastic resin glue—a brown powder that is mixed with water—most often. I have had good success with it over many years.

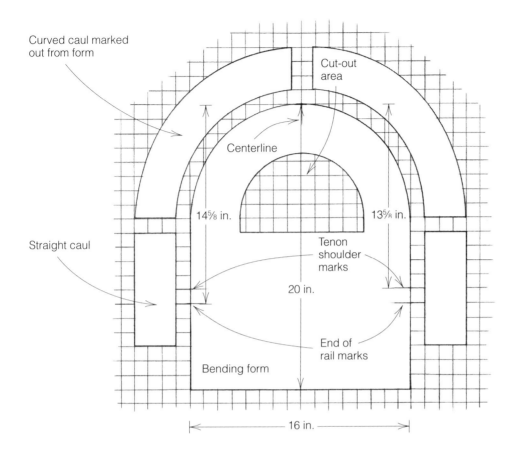

Curved caul marked out from form

Cut-out area

Centerline

14⅝ in.

13⅝ in.

Straight caul

Tenon shoulder marks

20 in.

End of rail marks

Bending form

16 in.

Making the bending form and cauls To set up for laminating the curved rail, you must start by making a bending form (see the drawing above). For this chair, it is important that the form be symmetrical. Making a pattern for half of the form and flipping it is a good way to ensure symmetry. Mark out however many layers of plywood, particleboard, or medium-density fiberboard (MDF) you need to get to a 2¾-in.- to 3-in.-thick form, then cut out the layers, and smooth one of them carefully, checking again for symmetry. (You can leave the cut-out area rough.) Screw and glue on the other layers one at a time, and flush-trim with a router to smooth them to exactly the same shape. Once assembled, sand

the edge to eliminate any remaining irregularities, and apply a coat of paste wax to prevent glue from sticking to the form. Finish up by marking the locations for the ends of the rail, tenon shoulders, and the centerline on the form (see the drawing above).

The cauls should be made from the bending form, not from a drawing, so that they're spaced the proper distance for gluing up the lamination. Start by making a disk that is twice the diameter of the desired thickness of the U-shaped rail—in this case, a 1-in.-thick rail means a 2-in.-diameter disk. Drill a small hole through the center of the disk, and with a pencil in the hole, roll the disk around the form, marking the inner shape of the

When marking the plywood for the bending cauls, trace around the form with a 2-in.-diameter disk. This will give you a line that is the proper distance from the form for clamping the rail.

cauls onto a piece of plywood, particleboard, or MDF (see the photo above). Cut and sand carefully to this line, then use a marking gauge to mark the outside of the caul about 3 in. to 4 in. away. (The dimensions are not critical.) Once the outside is cut, you can use the layer as a pattern for the other layers, which are then cut, attached, and flush-trimmed to shape to make a caul equal in thickness to the form. Cut the assembled caul apart on the centerline; it is much easier to work with two halves. Make up some separate straight cauls for the sides of the U-shaped rail out of ¾-in.- or 1-in.-thick stock. Cut an assortment of clamping spacer blocks, too. These should be 1¾ in. square and anywhere from 6 in. to 12 in. long.

Gluing up If this is the first time you're doing something like this, do a dry run—there's a lot to juggle. When you're ready, glue up the lamination on the floor or on a large, stable work surface. (Cover either with a tarp if you don't want glue all over.) Get everything you'll need together: paint roller (with a short nap or foam roller cover) and roller tray for the glue, spacer blocks, strips, forms, cauls, and clamps. Then mix up the glue. Wear a dust mask when mixing and gloves when handling the glue. I mix up 500 ml of the plastic resin powder with 200 ml of water, which is plenty. Lay the strips out on the swept floor or tarp, and spread glue with the paint roller on all but the last strip. (See the photos on the facing page for the steps that follow.)

Top left: The strips are all stacked up and centered on the form, ready for the lamination to begin.
Top right: An extra pair of hands (in this case, my dad's) is important when bending the strips around the form. I've done this without help, but it was very difficult.

Left: When clamping the cauls in place, be sure to align the mating ends with the centerline of the form.

All the clamps are in place. Notice how the spacer blocks work to create room in the middle for more clamps and how the clamps alternate between top and bottom.

Stack the strips back up in order, pull the bundle around the form, then place a clamp across the bottom to hold everything loosely in place. This will probably require an assistant, but don't wait until you're struggling to get the clamps on to try to find someone. Then work on clamping the cauls on the curve. Place clamps both above and underneath the assembly to ensure even pressure. (Lift the form up, and slide them in on the bottom.) Here is where you use some of the spacer blocks you made earlier to keep the clamps from running into each other (see the photo above). Finally,

clamp straight cauls on the parallel sides of the lamination. Once you've caught your breath (the first time doing one of these glue-ups is the hardest), transfer the marks for the ends of the rail and centerline onto the U-shaped rail.

Let the lamination sit in clamps at least overnight, then remove it from the form. Transfer the marks for the ends and the centerline to the inside face of the lamination before doing anything else.

Even though the lamination is not a straight board, it is still possible to joint an edge (see the photo above). This is hard on the jointer knives (or hand-plane irons); expect to find some nicks in the knives from the glue lines. I schedule work on laminated parts just before I change knives, if at all possible. Having straightened one edge, set the rip fence 2½ in. from the blade, and rip the other edge parallel on the table-saw. Attach a tall auxiliary fence to the rip fence so you have a large flat surface to help keep the lamination stable. Rip slowly and carefully (see the top photo on p. 154). Cut the lamination to length. Then mark out the tenons from the leg mortises as we have done throughout the book (see the photo essay on pp. 116-117), and cut the tenons with the tenon-

Rip the other edge of the lamination parallel to the jointed edge. Be sure to use a high fence for this cut.

After cutting the lamination to length, tenon the ends of the rail with the tenoning jig.

Cut the leg notches on the tablesaw using a support jig to help hold the curved rail and to locate the notches accurately.

ing jig (see the bottom photo on the facing page). Trim the tenon ends down, round them over, and check the fit. Then miter the inside edges so they don't interfere with the front rail tenons.

Cutting notches for the rear legs

The back of the U-shaped rail and the fronts of the rear legs are both notched to create a shallow lap joint. The legs are attached with screws, but the lap joints add significant strength. Lay out the notches in the rail symmetrically. Measure 5½ in. on a straight line to either side of the centerline of the curved rail, and mark these as the inside points of the rear legs (see the drawing on p. 148). The width of each notch should be the same thickness as the leg. Rather

than just pencil the lines for the notches square across the rail, scribe them with a knife. You can cut exactly to these lines with a chisel after the bulk of the waste for the notch has been removed.

The easiest way to remove this waste is on the tablesaw, using a support jig in conjunction with the miter gauge (see the sidebar on p. 156 to make the support jig). Screw an auxiliary fence to the miter gauge, and hold the support jig securely against this fence. Start with a shallow cut to be sure the cut is flat and straight (see the photo above). The full depth of the notch is only ⅛ in. Don't cut all the way to the scribed lines, but try to cut within 1/32 in. (See a discussion of this on p. 174.) Then test the fit of some milled leg stock in the notches. When the notches are the correct width, drill three pilot holes (arranged in a triangle pattern) for each leg. Drill first from the outside (in the notches) in. Then countersink the holes from the inside of the U-shaped rail.

Cutting and tenoning the front rail

The front rail is simply cut to size and tenoned. But you should check the length of the rail by assembling the U-shaped rail and the two front legs. The front rail should be about ⅛ in. wider between tenons than the actual distance between the front legs. This springs the U-shaped rail

---

SUPPORT JIG FOR CUTTING NOTCHES IN A U-SHAPED RAIL

When used with the miter gauge on the tablesaw, this support jig makes it easy to notch out the rail for the rear legs. To make the support jig, start by marking out the locations for the notches on the U-shaped rail (see "Cutting notches for the rear legs" on p. 155). Then make a support piece to hold the rail at the correct angle for notching, using a piece of 9-in. by 18-in. plywood. Draw

a line ½ in. up from and parallel to a long edge of the plywood. Place the U-shaped rail on the plywood with the notch location marks lined up with the marked line on the plywood. Trace the outside of the rail onto the plywood and bandsaw. Tack or screw the support piece to a 10-in. by 18-in. piece of plywood (see the drawing below).

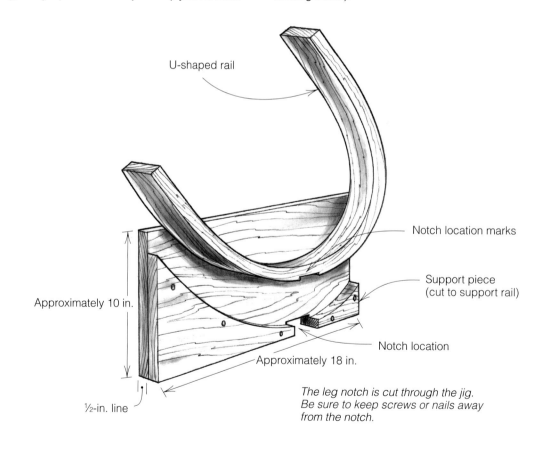

U-shaped rail

Notch location marks

Support piece
(cut to support rail)

Approximately 10 in.

Notch location

Approximately 18 in.

½-in. line

The leg notch is cut through the jig. Be sure to keep screws or nails away from the notch.

open a little, and the slight tension that results helps to hold the joints together.

MAKING THE BACK ASSEMBLY

The back assembly calls for some different joinery methods because the legs are at a steep angle to each other, and the slats are tilted to different angles to follow the curve of the spine. Even with these different methods of joinery, the same basic principles guide the work.

Making the rear legs

As with many of the other chairs in this book, you can cut the rear legs to shape either before or after cutting the mortises. Rectangular blanks are not necessary, however. You can mark out the legs with the rail flats aligned with the jointed edge of a board, and cut only the back side of the leg to shape. This makes it much simpler to cut the lower slat mortise and the notch for the lap joint with the curved rail. If you opt to cut the legs entirely to shape first, the usual advice applies. Establish the rail flats first. Then rout the lower slat mortise with a mortising template. For the notches, support the leg at the correct angle (with a cutoff or a block cut for this purpose) to give a wider and more stable base so that the leg can be safely and accurately handled on the tablesaw.

Whichever method you choose, start by making a ¼-in.-plywood pattern for the rear legs from the drawing at right. The wood for the legs should be milled to 1⅝ in. thick (1¾ in. will also work). Joint one or both edges, and lay out the legs with the rail flats carefully aligned with the edge(s). Cut out only the back curve of the legs. Cut the ⅛-in.-deep notch for the curved rail on the

PATTERN FOR REAR LEGS

Scale: 1 square = 1 in.

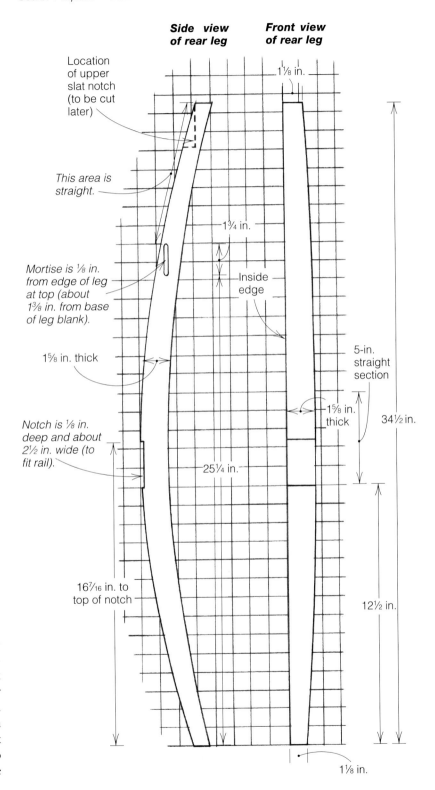

Side view of rear leg

Front view of rear leg

Location of upper slat notch (to be cut later)

This area is straight.

Mortise is ⅛ in. from edge of leg at top (about 1⅜ in. from base of leg blank).

1⅝ in. thick

Notch is ⅛ in. deep and about 2½ in. wide (to fit rail).

16⁷⁄₁₆ in. to top of notch

1⅛ in.

1¾ in.

Inside edge

25¼ in.

5-in. straight section

1⅝ in. thick

34½ in.

12½ in.

1⅛ in.

FRONT LEG PATTERN WITH MORTISE LOCATION

Scale: 1 square = 1 in.

Front leg

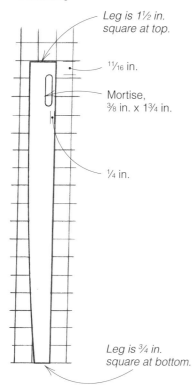

Leg is 1½ in.
square at top.

¹¹⁄₁₆ in.

Mortise,
⅜ in. x 1¾ in.

¼ in.

Leg is ¾ in.
square at bottom.

tablesaw using the miter gauge with an auxiliary fence attached. Carefully check the fit of the rail in this notch. Then locate and rout the ¼-in. by 1¾-in. mortise for the lower slat, using the router fence (see the drawing on p. 157).

Cut the fronts of the legs to shape, and smooth. The top 9 in. of the fronts of the legs are a straight line and should be planed carefully to maintain this.

Dry-assemble the front legs, the front rail, and the curved rail, and screw with 2-in. drywall screws or clamp the rear legs into place. There

is more work to do on the legs, but it must wait until after we deal with the slats.

Making the slats

The two slats are joined to the legs differently. Work on the lower slat first because this is harder to adjust later. For this slat, we'll use floating (or loose) tenons. It's easier to locate the joints correctly, and it also results in a stronger joint because the grain doesn't run across the tenon on as steep an angle as it would with a regular tenon.

Making the lower slat Start work on the lower slat by determining the angle for the ends of the slat

MARKING MORTISE LOCATIONS

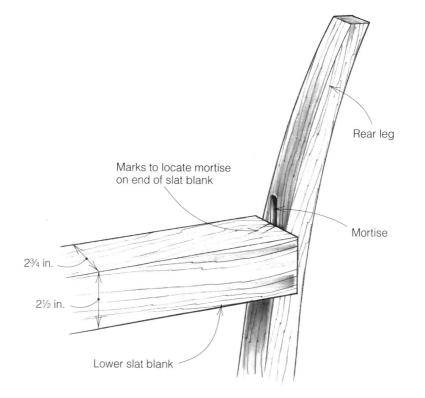

Marks to locate mortise
on end of slat blank

Rear leg

Mortise

2¾ in.

2½ in.

Lower slat blank

blank. Set a straightedge across the fronts of the legs at the same height on both legs. With a bevel gauge, set the angle between the straightedge and the inside face of the leg. Check both legs. If they are not the same, it's better to deal with each angle individually. I've tried splitting the difference, but it usually leads to headaches later. While you're at it, measure and note the distance between the legs ⅜ in. down from the mortises (that is, at the bottom of the slat) at the front inside corner.

Before starting on the actual slat, make a test pattern. Lay out the appropriate angle(s) the measured distance apart, then cut. Check the fit by holding the pattern at the bottom of the slat height, and make any necessary adjustments.

Once the test pattern fits well between the legs, mill up the slat blank 2½ in. wide by 2¾ in. deep by about 15 in. long. Cut the angle(s) on the ends, leaving the correct distance between them. Locate the mortises on the blank by holding it in place between the legs so that some of the leg mortises are visible. Mark these locations to the blank, and transfer the marks to the ends of the blank (see the bottom drawing on the facing page).

Routing the mortises combines template mortising with a holding setup like the tenoning jig. In fact, the tenoning jig can be used. I found it quicker to make up a separate jig that is a little easier to work with, however (see the drawing at right for how to set up the jig). In use, the angled end of the slat blank is clamped flush with the underside of the jig, with the mortise location centered under the mortising template. Adjust the template back and forth until the slot is centered on the blank. Cut the mortises with the

MORTISE-CUTTING JIG

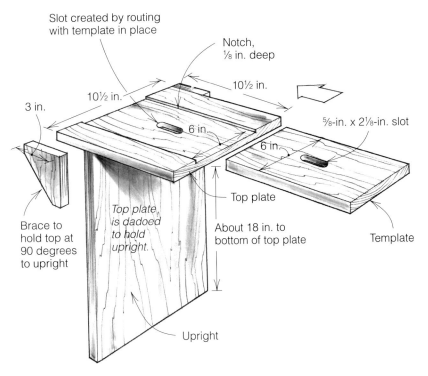

Slot created by routing with template in place

Notch, ⅛ in. deep

10½ in.

10½ in.

3 in.

6 in.

⅝-in. x 2⅛-in. slot

6 in.

Brace to hold top at 90 degrees to upright

Top plate is dadoed to hold upright.

Top plate

About 18 in. to bottom of top plate

Template

Upright

Mortise-cutting jig in use

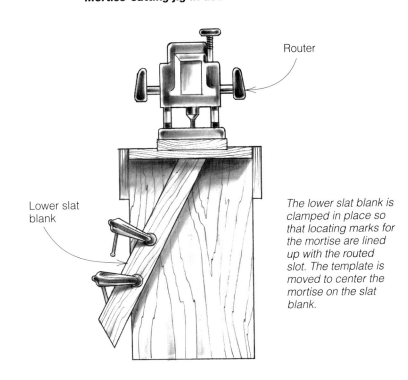

Router

Lower slat blank

The lower slat blank is clamped in place so that locating marks for the mortise are lined up with the routed slot. The template is moved to center the mortise on the slat blank.

Front view

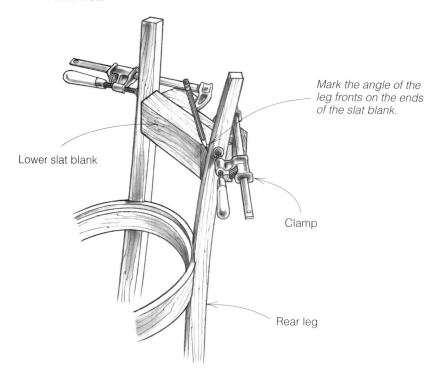

Mark the angle of the leg fronts on the ends of the slat blank.

Lower slat blank

Clamp

Rear leg

Top view

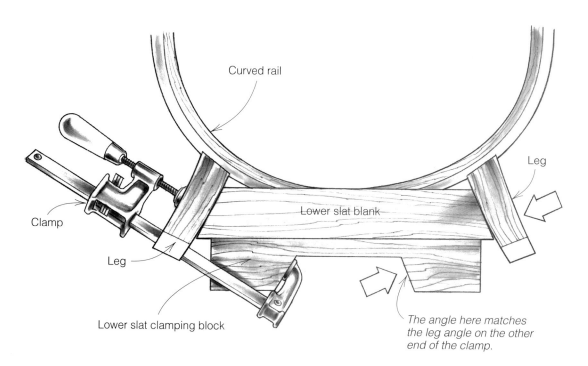

Curved rail

Leg

Lower slat blank

Clamp

Leg

Lower slat clamping block

The angle here matches the leg angle on the other end of the clamp.

The lower slat is clamped in place. Note the cutoff between the clamping block and the slat. The upper slat notches have already been cut in this photo.

plunge router and a ¼-in. straight bit. The depth of the mortise should not exceed ⅝ in., or you risk cutting into the mortise when shaping the back of the slat.

Once both mortises are cut, mill up some tenon stock. One of the peculiarities of the floating tenon is that mortises cut in end grain and in long grain may differ slightly in size even if they are cut exactly the same way. When milling up the tenon stock, check the fit in both the leg and slat mortises. If there is any difference between mortises, mill for a tight fit in the looser mortise, and fit the tenon to the tighter one after the tenons are cut to length. Cut the tenon stock to length (the combined depths of the mortises less ¹⁄₃₂ in.), and test-fit the slat with the legs. To get an accurate idea of the fit, clamp the joints tight. Make a simple clamping block with a notch in the

middle that has the leg angles on either side of the notch (see the drawing on the facing page).

With the slat clamped in place between the legs, mark the angle of the fronts of the legs onto the ends of the slat blank. Disassemble the legs and slat, and using a pattern for the slat (with an 18-in.-radius curve on the inside), mark the curve on top of the slat, recessed about ¹⁄₁₆ in. to ⅛ in. behind the fronts of the legs as just marked. Tilt the bandsaw table so it cuts the marked angle on the end of the slat blank, then saw out the curved shape of the slat.

Reassemble the legs and slat with the front assembly. Take the cutoff from the back of the slat, trim a little bit off each end, and tack the clamping block to it, so you can clamp the joints tightly (see the photo above). Now start on the upper slat.

Top view

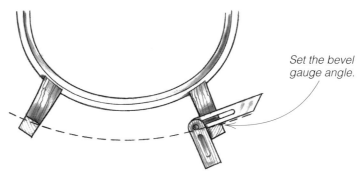

Set the bevel
gauge angle.

**First cut in
notching jig**

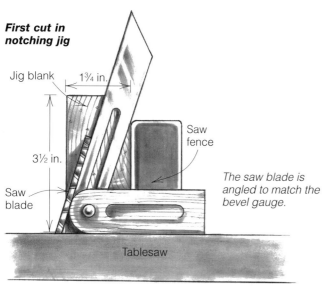

Jig blank

1¾ in.

3½ in.

Saw
blade

Saw
fence

Tablesaw

The saw blade is
angled to match the
bevel gauge.

**Second cut in
notching jig**

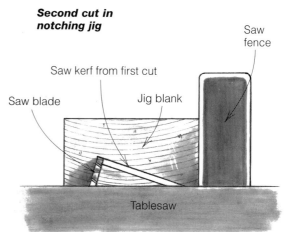

Saw kerf from first cut

Saw blade

Jig blank

Saw
fence

Tablesaw

Holding jig for left leg

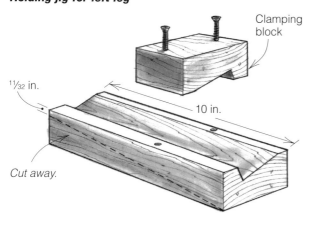

Clamping
block

11/32 in.

10 in.

Cut away.

Holding jig for right leg

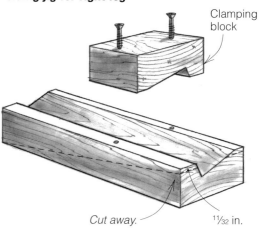

Clamping
block

Cut away.

11/32 in.

Making the upper slat The first step in fitting the upper slat is to cut an odd-shaped notch in the upper part of the legs. Cutting this notch is the most complicated part of making this chair, although it is not difficult to do. The notch is at a compound angle to the leg. To calculate the first of the two angles (actually there are three angles to worry about, but we'll deal with the third later), make up a plywood pattern for the curve of the back slat. I settled on a radius of 18½ in. for the outside (the back) of the slat. For now, this is the only curve that matters. Cut out the pattern, and carefully smooth it.

Trace the pattern onto the tops of the legs, lining up the pattern from inside corner to inside corner. With a bevel gauge held against the inside faces of the legs, line up the blade of the gauge with the lines just drawn (see the drawing on the facing page). Even though you drew a curve, it is shallow enough to treat as a line. Test out the angle on top of both legs to be sure it is the same. If the angle is different, you'll have to make up separate holding jigs, each with the proper angle (see below).

The notches are cut on the tablesaw using two jigs–one for each leg–that incorporate the angle just found. To make the jigs, start with a scrap of wood 1¾ in. thick, 3½ in. wide, and 28 in. long (or two pieces 14 in. long, if you have different angles on the two legs). Cut an angled trough on the wide face of the block by setting the blade on the tablesaw to the bevel gauge angle (see the drawing on the facing page). Make the first cut with the blade high and the block on edge; make the second cut with the block on the just-cut face and the blade lowered to complete the notch. Cut the block into two 10-in.-long pieces and two 3-in.- to 4-in.-long pieces.

The secondary angle is one I determined to be 9 degrees by experimenting with the chair's comfort. This is best laid out by marking a line on the edge of the block from a point $^{11}/_{32}$ in. down from one of the top corners to the opposite bottom corner. Set both blocks in front of you, with the steeper part of the notch closest to you. Mark one block so that it angles from top left to bottom right. This will be for the left leg (on your left when sitting in the chair). Mark the other block from top right to bottom left for the right leg. Bandsaw both blocks, and smooth the bandsawn surfaces if they are rough or bumpy.

To complete the holding jigs, drill two oversize pilot holes for screws on top and near the sides of the 4-in. pieces so they can be used as clamping blocks (see the bottom drawings on the facing page).

Mark the bottom of the notches on the right side of the left leg and the left side of the right leg, 2½ in. down from the tops of the legs. Set up for cutting a notch by laying a leg in the appropriate holding jig with the mark for the bottom of the notch lined up with the corner on the high side of the jig. Screw the clamp block down, then make sure the leg is seated correctly. Note that both holding blocks are used with the thicker end of the wedge toward the blade. Raise the blade (dado or regular) so that it just touches the inside corner of the top of the leg (the front corner on the right leg and the back corner on the left leg), and cut the notch with multiple passes over the blade until you reach the bottom mark (see the photo on p. 164). Be sure to hold the jig firmly down on the saw table at all times. When you switch to the other leg, be sure to check the height of the blade because you may need to adjust it.

I'm just beginning to cut an upper slat notch with the leg held in the notching jig.

Now mark out and cut the upper slat. You'll need a board 3¼ in. thick, 3½ in. wide, and 21 in. long. (It is also possible to make the upper slat as a lamination, which is a much easier lamination than the U-shaped rail.)

Before proceeding with fitting the upper slat or with eliminating the small gap formed by the bottom of the slat and the leg notch (the third angle mentioned above), it is time to taper the outside faces of the rear legs. Legs are usually tapered on the inside faces, but tapering the outside narrows the legs where they need to be narrowed, and you really can't tell the difference in this case. Taper both bottom and top of the leg to a thickness of 1⅛ in. I made up a flexible pattern from some thick veneer left over from bending. Cut the tapers on the bandsaw as gentle curves, then plane, scrape, and/or

sand smooth. Leave the areas around the seat notches straight to avoid gaps in the joint.

Now smooth the slat itself—or at least the outside. With the lower slat clamped tight, check the fit of the upper slat, and note where the biggest problems are. The best way to get a good fit is to sand the notch using the slat itself as a sanding block. But unless the fit is near perfect to start, you should pare away some wood from the high spots. Don't remove wood out at the edges at all; instead pare a hollow in the center of the notch. Then stick an 80-grit sanding disk (with pressure-sensitive adhesive) on the back of the slat about where it will fit into the notch. I put mine about two-thirds of the way onto the slat, and cut off the extra with a utility knife. Put the slat in both notches, and

You can get a precise fit by sanding the notch to fit the slat.

sand with a motion that keeps the slat riding against the notches (see the photo above).

Check your progress often, alternating between sanding and paring away waste from the center. When one side fits, move on to the other. The result should be a perfect fit. Use this same method to fit the bottom of the notch tightly to the slat, but use more downward pressure (and put the sandpaper on the bottom of the slat).

Before drilling the countersunk holes for the 1-in. drywall screws that attach the legs to the slat, plane the tops of the legs parallel to the notches. This is strictly for looks—it gets rid of the awkward angles there. With the plane or a sanding block, ease the transition from the planed section to the rest of the leg.

Smooth the inside of the slat if you haven't already done so, then cut the slat to length. Leave ⅞ in. to 1 in. to the outside of the legs, and cut the ends off at a 6-degree angle, wider at the top to complement the flare of the legs.

Lay out and counterbore pilot holes in the back of each leg for attaching the slat, and temporarily screw the slat into place (don't glue yet).

PREPARING FOR THE SLIP SEAT

Cutting the recess for the slip seat is a three-step process. First, rabbet the U-shaped rail about ¼ in. deep with a ½-in. rabbeting bit, taking a light cut. This should leave a ⅜-in. to ½-in. lip, depending on the thickness of the curved rail. Rabbet the front rail on the tablesaw, and leave the same size lip. Then rout away the waste at the top of the front legs with a flush-trimming template (see p. 46 for more details).

To mark out the slip-seat blank, dry-assemble the U-shaped rail, the front legs, and the front rail, and set the subassembly upside down on a piece of ⅜-in. or ½-in. plywood. Trace around the outside of the rail assembly, and cut the plywood to shape. Mark a line ⅝ in. in from the just-cut edges, and cut to this line. Then test the fit in the slip seat recess, and adjust so there is an even gap of at least ¹⁄₁₆ in. all around to accommodate the fabric used to upholster the seat. (Make the gap bigger for thicker fabrics.) Sand the edges smooth and ease all of the corners. Send the seat to the upholsterer, or do the job yourself (see the sidebar on pp. 84-85).

Cut and fit a pair of corner blocks for the front, and temporarily screw them into place so you can mark and drill both seat blank and corner blocks for the 8-32 T-nuts and bolts. In the back where there are no corners or corner blocks, screw a small block to the center of the rail, and drill it (and the seat) for a T-nut and bolt. Then disassemble everything, and move on to final shaping and smoothing.

SHAPING AND SMOOTHING THE PARTS

Parts of the chair have been shaped and smoothed, but it's time to go over everything prior to assembly. Plane, scrape, and/or sand all surfaces, and work carefully on the twist at the top of the rear legs. Carefully sand the exposed end grain at the top of the legs. Round the back edges of the rear legs with a ¼-in. roundover bit. The twist at the top will interfere with routing all the way to the top of the leg, so finish rounding at the top with sandpaper. Chamfer the front edges of the rear legs. This adds a little more interest to the shape of the legs and reflects the square front and round back of the completed chair. Round over the edges of the lower slat with a rasp and sandpaper. (The angles rule out the use of the router.) Some of the edges of the upper slat can be routed, but not all. Be especially careful with the lower back edge. Don't round over where the slat meets the leg notch or there will be a gap. Instead, mark the locations of the legs on the slat, and rout close to the marks. Then sand symmetrical transitions from the roundovers to the flats.

ASSEMBLING THE PARTS

You'll need to make one more caul prior to assembly, which will help you glue the U-shaped rail to the front legs and rail (see the photo on the facing page). Trace the shape of the back 4½ in. of the U-shaped rail onto a piece of ¾-in. plywood roughly 18 in. by 6 in., and cut out the curve to create the caul. Smooth this carefully, then add another ¾-in.-thick layer and flush-trim. Once this is done, gather together all of the clamps, clamp pads, glue, screws, the lower back slat caul, along with the chair parts in preparation for the glue-up.

Clamping the U-shaped rail to the front legs and rail would be very difficult without this caul, which is cut to match the shape of the U-shaped rail.

Here again, glue-up is best done in stages. Start with the front legs and front rail. Spread glue in the mortises and lightly on the tenons, insert fillers into the side mortises to keep from crushing them when clamping, and clamp the front together. When dry, set up to clamp the U-shaped rail to the front legs. This is easier with the legs and rail upside down. Glue, then clamp using the U-shaped rail caul, and tighten the clamps evenly.

Using 2-in. drywall screws, screw and glue one of the rear legs to the rail, then attach the lower slat and the other leg. Hold the slat caul in place in the center of the slat with a clamp, then clamp the legs tightly to the slat. After all of this, the upper slat is easy—just glue and screw it into place. Then cut plugs for the screw holes, glue them into place, and cut and sand them off flush and smooth. Reattach the corner blocks.

FINISHING UP

Turn the chair over, and tack on some glides. Apply your choice of finish (see the appendix on p. 195 for a description of the oil and wax finish that I prefer). When the finish is dry, attach the upholstered slip seat. Admire your work on this comfortable, elegant, and challenging chair. You've got a start on your own small café.

CAPTAIN'S CHAIR

This captain's chair is both very different from previous chairs in this book and also a logical extension of what we've done so far. It is quite different in structure. The other chairs are all based at least in part on a framework that joins the legs together with rails. On this chair, the legs are attached to a solid plank seat. The joinery here is essential, but screws are equally responsible for holding the parts together.

This is also the first armchair in the book. Arms are a necessary part of this chair's structure, linking the front and rear legs. And even though there is a solid joint between the seat and legs, the front leg must extend well above the level of the seat for this joint to work well.

It is hard to make a chair like this without acknowledging the influence of Sam Maloof (see the photo on p. 25). Although there are many other chairs of this basic structure with legs screwed to a plank seat, Maloof's seem to define the genre. So even though the joinery and shape on all of these chairs (including this one) may be different, most are all offsprings of his designs. This type of chair has a lot of appeal. It allows for a great deal of design and shaping freedom, and the structure is still uncomplicated and unobtrusive.

One last point before we start on the chair. With more shaping to do, the comfort and final look of the chair are largely in your hands. I will discuss how to saddle a seat for comfort, but you have to work the seat, sit on it, and work it some more, over and over again until you are satisfied with the results. Most of the edges are rounded over, but you could change the look of the piece by treating the edges and the transitions between parts differently from the way I've done it.

BUILDING THE STRUCTURE

This chair is made in two phases: building the structure and then shaping all of the parts. Some of the shaping will be done on the individual parts, but a lot of the shaping work requires that the chair be together.

Before beginning, make up a set of patterns for the chair parts out of ¼-in. plywood (see the drawing on pp. 170-171).

Front view

Side view

The shoulder of the tenon
angles back 2 degrees.

Back slat detail

Scale: 1 square = 1 in.

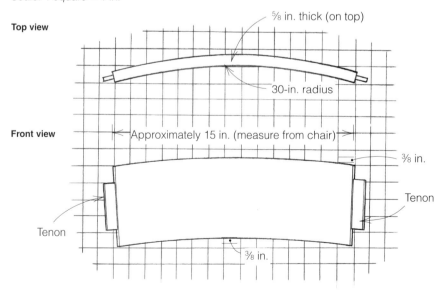

Top view

⅝ in. thick (on top)

30-in. radius

Front view

Approximately 15 in. (measure from chair)

⅜ in.

Tenon

Tenon

⅜ in.

Leg detail

Scale: 1 square = 1 in.

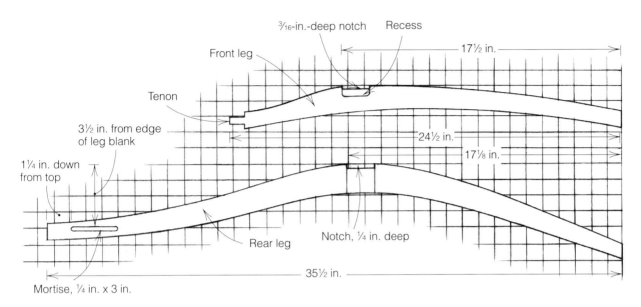

³⁄₁₆-in.-deep notch
Recess
Front leg
17½ in.
Tenon
3½ in. from edge of leg blank
24½ in.
17⅛ in.
1¼ in. down from top
Rear leg
Notch, ¼ in. deep
35½ in.
Mortise, ¼ in. x 3 in.

Seat detail

Scale: 1 square = 1 in.

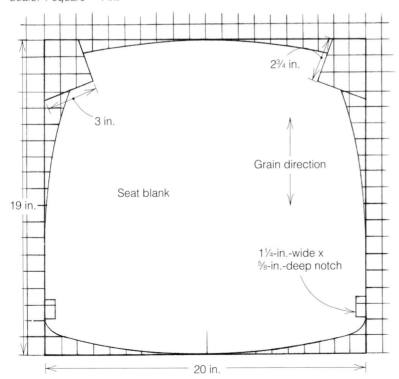

2¾ in.
3 in.
Grain direction
Seat blank
19 in.
1¼-in.-wide x ⅝-in.-deep notch
20 in.

Arm detail

This is an approximation of the arm back. See the text for how to work out the exact angle.

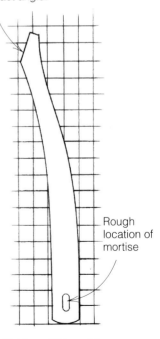

Rough location of mortise

Cut from 18-in. x 4-in. x 1⅛-in.-thick blank.

Making the plank seat

Mill (or purchase) the 1¾-in.-thick lumber for the seat. The seat is best glued up out of four boards, all from the same piece of wood, if possible. The choice of wood is not one to take lightly. A wood that is easier to shape will cut hours off the overall time spent on this project. I have occasionally carved seats out of hard maple. I usually curse my way through the carving and smoothing, but the finished chair is incredibly smooth to the touch. I much prefer to work walnut or mahogany, with cherry coming in a distant third.

Cut the seat boards to size, joint the edges, and glue up the seat blank. Then sand the bottom of the blank, and cut it to 20 in. wide and 19 in. deep. (The grain runs from front to back.)

The legs attach to the seat with interlocking notches, which are mostly cut on the tablesaw (see the drawings below and on p. 171). For the front leg notches, start by rounding over the top and bottom edges of the seat where the front legs attach with a ¼-in. roundover bit. (This could also be done after the notches are cut; just be careful not to "fall" into the notches.) Then mark out the notches on the top and on the bottom of the blank, and cut them on the tablesaw. Note that the width of the notches is ¼ in. less than the thickness of the legs. As a shortcut, you can use a stop on the miter gauge (or

FRONT AND REAR LEG JOINTS

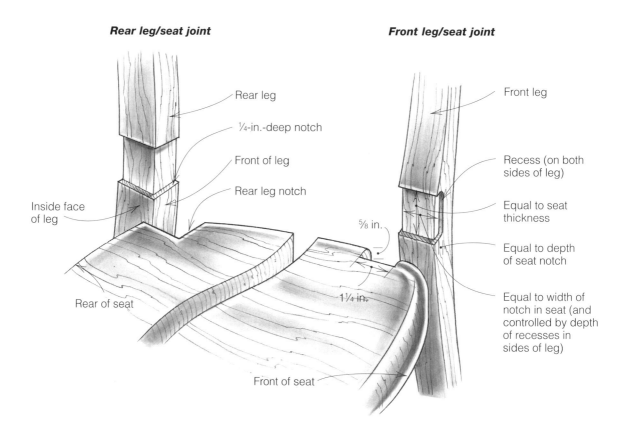

Rear leg/seat joint

Rear leg
¼-in.-deep notch
Front of leg
Rear leg notch
Inside face of leg
Rear of seat

Front leg/seat joint

Front leg
Recess (on both sides of leg)
Equal to seat thickness
Equal to depth of seat notch
Equal to width of notch in seat (and controlled by depth of recesses in sides of leg)
⅝ in.
1¼ in.
Front of seat

When cutting the front leg notches in the seat, use the rip fence to help locate the notches in exactly the same place. It's not visible, but the miter gauge does have a high auxiliary fence attached.

I extended the auxiliary fence past the blade to make this cut for the rear leg notch because my miter gauge only works on the left side.

the rip fence) when cutting one notch, then flip the seat blank over and cut the other side at the same setting (see the left photo above). Attach a tall auxiliary fence to the miter gauge when cutting the notches—it's both easier and safer. A dado blade speeds up the task but isn't necessary; multiple passes with an ordinary saw blade will do the job, too. Clean up the bottoms of the notches with a chisel if they aren't smooth.

The rear leg notches are also cut on the tablesaw, but with the regular blade raised up and tilted 15 degrees (from 90 degrees)—I call this the splay angle. (I've provided this angle because you'll need it later for the

chair back slat.) Make the cuts in the sides first, then make the cuts in the back of the seat. For the latter, you'll have to rotate the seat so that it is on the far side of the blade— either set up the miter guide on the other side, or extend the auxiliary fence across the blade to support the seat adequately (see the right photo above). If your saw doesn't have a 3-in. depth of cut, just bandsaw the notches carefully, and clean them up with a chisel.

Now trace the seat pattern onto the seat blank. Bandsaw the blank roughly to shape, but leave the back of the seat uncut for now. Save the cutoffs for use later.

The seat notches on the front (shown) and rear legs are cut on the tablesaw.

the location and size on the inside faces of the legs, then transfer the marks around to the sides so you can see them when cutting. Then cut the notches ¼ in. deep on the tablesaw (see the photo at left).

To complete the joint, cut the recesses on the sides of the front legs (see the drawing on p. 172). This looks better than a simple lap joint and allows the visible part of the joint to remain tight even if you have to do some fitting in the notch (see the photo on the facing page). Make up a jig for template routing the recesses (see the drawing on the facing page), then set the depth of cut so that the remaining leg section fits tightly into the seat notch. (The cuts should be about ⅛ in. deep.) Rout both sides of the legs.

Before testing the fit, relieve the outside corners of the seat notches just a little so they don't split off when inserting and removing the legs. Adjust the depth of the routed areas as necessary for a tight fit. Cut the legs to shape. Then cut a curved taper on the inside faces of each leg both above and below the notch with the bandsaw.

The rear legs are easier than the front legs because the notches are much less complex. Lay out the legs with the notch flat of the pattern carefully lined up with the edge of the board. With the pattern in place, check the distance from the edge of the board to the bottom of the leg pattern to be sure that both legs will be the same. Then trace the pattern, but don't cut it to shape yet. Measure the thickness of the seat blank on both sides of the chair, then mark out the legs accordingly. The top of the seat should be the same height on both legs, and any discrepancies should be at the bottom of the notch. On the tablesaw cut the ¼-in.-

Making the legs

On this chair, the legs should either be cut from rectangular blanks or from a board where the inside of the leg is aligned with a straight edge so the notches can be cut on the tablesaw. There is also some routing that will reference off the straight edge. Mill up the leg stock to 1½ in. thick. Start with the front legs (see the Leg detail in the drawing on p. 171). Cut the rectangular blanks to size, or cut out the outside edge of the legs, and leave the inside edge straight (as I did). Then cut the tenons for the arms on the top of the legs with the tenoning jig. Use a narrow wedge to tilt each leg sideways in the jig so that the tenon shoulder angles back 2 degrees. I give this as an angle because once again, the amount of tilt is not critical—I just like the look of the chair better with the arms angled down a little toward the back. Remember that the left and right legs must be tilted in opposite directions.

Work on the interlocking notches next. Measure the thickness of the seat blank at each notch, mark out deep notches on both the front and inside faces of the blank, and check to be sure the leg fits snugly onto the seat notch. Then rout the mortises for the back slat using the plunge router and fence. The mortises are parallel to the edge of the leg blank to avoid having to cut the slat tenons at a compound angle (more on this later). Cut the rear legs to shape, and cut a curved taper below the notch.

Dry-assemble the legs and the seat blank, counterbore pilot holes for the 2½-in. drywall screws that will hold the chair together, and then temporarily screw the chair together. Mark the seat blank where it meets the legs so you can reshape the seat to the legs later.

This is the goal: a finished front-leg-to-seat joint.

A ROUTER TEMPLATE FOR CUTTING RECESSES

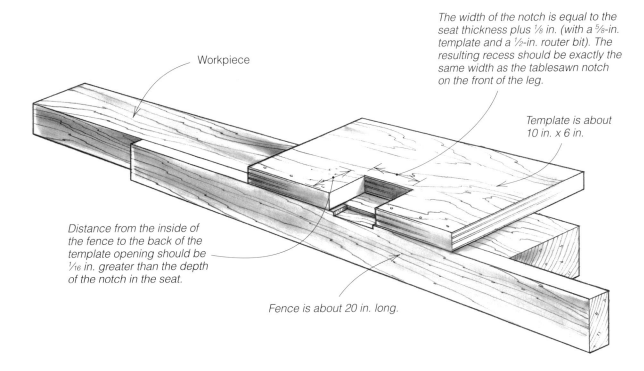

Workpiece

The width of the notch is equal to the seat thickness plus ⅛ in. (with a ⅝-in. template and a ½-in. router bit). The resulting recess should be exactly the same width as the tablesawn notch on the front of the leg.

Template is about 10 in. x 6 in.

Distance from the inside of the fence to the back of the template opening should be ¹⁄₁₆ in. greater than the depth of the notch in the seat.

Fence is about 20 in. long.

To determine the exact angle for the arms and the mortise location, make a sizing pattern. I'm marking the pattern here for the angle for the back of the arm.

Making the arms

The arms also start as rectangular blanks. But before you start work on the blanks, you need to make a sizing pattern to determine the mortise location and the angle where the arm joins the rear leg. Cut the pattern from 1/4-in. plywood, and saw a slot 3/8 in. wide, 5 1/2 in. long, and 7/8 in. from the edge in the end. Place the slot over the front leg tenon, and slide the pattern back until it just touches the rear leg. Mark the rear leg angle on the pattern using a stick about 3/8 in. thick to get the proper space (see the photo at left).

Remove the pattern, cut the angle, and replace it, checking to see if the angle is right and if the angled section is wide enough for the joint with the leg. (Because the leg curves back, the arm needs to extend behind the leg.) With the angled part of the pattern snug against the rear leg, mark the locations for the mortise—about 1/16 in. forward of the actual location—and for the rear end of the arm—about 1/4 in. behind the back of the leg. Transfer this information to the underside of the appropriate arm blank, rout the mortise with the plunge router and fence, and cut the angle on the back end of the arm. Repeat the process, flipping the pattern over for the other side of the chair.

Now mark and cut the arms to shape. Fit the tenons to the mortises, and put the arms into place on the front legs. It may be a tight fit because there is a little extra wood on the back of the arms, but you can work them into place. Clamp the arms tightly to the front legs, then scribe lines both top and bottom where the arms touch the rear legs to locate the shallow notches that will help secure the arms in place there. Routing the notches can be done freehand or with a simple jig.

I actually find it quicker to rout by eye close to the scribed lines, then clean up with a chisel (see the sidebar on the facing page).

For a jig, cut a notch roughly 3 in. long and 1/8 in. wider than the arm thickness (this should also be the distance between the scribed lines) in a scrap of plywood. Clamp this into place on the side of the leg with the scribed lines centered between the sides of the notch, then rout with a 1/2-in. bit and a 5/8-in. guide bushing.

To prevent tearout on the edges of the leg, rout with a light climb cut to score both inside and outside edges, then rout away the waste. Once the notches are cut and the arms fit, slip the arms into place, and counterbore pilot holes for the screws that will hold the arms in the notches. Mark lines on the insides of the arms where they meet the legs so you can get a start on shaping the arms, and trim the backs of the arms roughly flush with the backs of the legs. The final smoothing of these areas should wait until after assembly.

Making the back slat

Though the joinery for the back slat appears to have compound angles, we'll cut the tenons as simple angles in a thicker slat blank, then bandsaw the curve at the appropriate angle to create the desired effect (as in Chapter 8). To cut a tenon in a piece as wide as the back slat in the tenoning jig described in Chapter 2, you'll need a modified template with a wider opening. To enable you to cut the 1/4-in. tenons with the 1/4-in.-thick template bar, you'll also need to switch from the 1/2-in. bit with 5/8-in. guide bushing to a flush-trimming bit with the bearing located above the cutting edges. Note that the range of the depth of cut is limited—the bearing must ride on the bar on the tenoning template. Be sure not to

SIZING THE NOTCHES PRECISELY

To go from a knife line to a perfectly straight, chiseled edge requires a little knowledge of chisel technique, but less virtuoso skill than you might think. The main problem when trying to chisel exactly to a line is that the chisel "backs up"–the beveled side of the chisel pushes the flat side back as the edge is forced into the wood. Two things are needed to eliminate this tendency: A place for the wood that you want to remove to go (in this case, into the routed notch), and some wood to support the flat of the chisel (see the drawing below). The key here is to relieve the knife line by gently chiseling out a small wedge of wood to the waste side of the line. (If there is more than 1/32 in. or so to chisel, make some preliminary cuts so the chiseled waste is easily pushed into the notch.) This leaves a very small shoulder to place the chisel against (see the photo at right). This helps to keep the individual chisel cuts exactly in line and also keeps the chisel from backing up.

Relieving a knife line makes it possible to chisel exactly to the line.

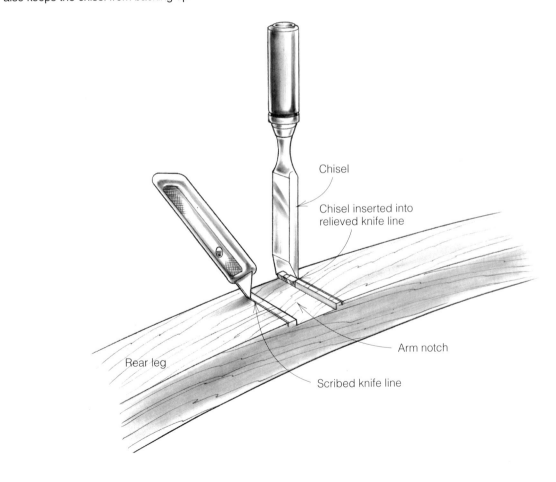

Chisel

Chisel inserted into relieved knife line

Arm notch

Rear leg

Scribed knife line

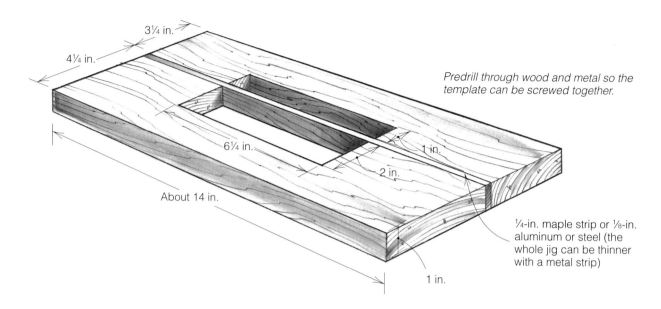

3¼ in.

4¼ in.

Predrill through wood and metal so the template can be screwed together.

6¼ in.

1 in.

2 in.

About 14 in.

¼-in. maple strip or ⅛-in. aluminum or steel (the whole jig can be thinner with a metal strip)

1 in.

plunge into the template. Since a new tenoning template is necessary, you could just make it with an ⅛-in.-wide and 1-in.-thick template bar made from aluminum or steel (see the drawing above). This would allow you to use the usual ½-in. bit and ⅝-in. guide bushing.

To begin work on the slat, measure the distance between the legs even with the bottom of the mortises and at a point ½ in. in front of them. Use this as the distance between tenons on the narrower side of the slat. Cut the back slat blank from stock that is 2 in. thick, 5¼ in. wide, and about 17 in. long. The tenon angle is the same as the splay angle—the angle you used to notch the seat for the rear legs (see p. 173). You'll need to calculate the "master" angle (90 degrees less the splay angle), and make a master-angle wedge to position the slat in the tenoning jig. Cut the tenon on one side, mark out the between-tenon distance, then cut the other side. Remove the arms and one of

the rear legs, then fit the slat into place, and reattach the leg. Check the fit of the slat, then mark out the shape of the rear legs (both front and back) on the ends of the slat. Use the marks from the front of the leg to set the angle of the bandsaw for cutting the curve of the slat. Then mark out the curve on the top edge (about a 30-in. radius for the front of the slat) so the slat will be recessed about ⅛ in. from the legs (and the leg marks). Bandsaw the front of the slat to shape, reset the saw to the angle of the mark from the back of the leg, and saw the back of the slat. Set aside the cutoffs to use for further shaping and smoothing. Then replace the slat in the chair, attach the arms, and have a seat.

SHAPING THE PARTS

The structure of the chair is now complete. What remains to be done is a process that requires different tools and a different approach from what we have done thus far in the

Start sculpting the seat by removing wood from the tail bones (rear portion of the seat). Here it's being done with a scooping plane.

book. This also opens up a whole area for personal expression, an opportunity to make the chair uniquely your own. It might be better to make one as I suggest before breaking new ground, however.

Making the seat

Of all the shaping on this chair, the sculpting of the seat is the most important to the comfort and visual impact of the chair. Sculpting a seat is hard work, but it's also very satisfying—and a lot of fun. You'll need a few special tools—with the current popularity of making Windsor chairs, there is a wide variety of tools available just for this task. I use two: a scooping plane and an inshave (or scorp). The scooping plane is a wood-bodied plane with a sole that is radiused both from front to back and from side to side. The iron is also radiused. You cup the plane in your hands and push it—usually across the grain at an angle. I use the plane for

roughing out the seat contour, then I switch to the inshave with its gentler curve to smooth out the bumpy surface left by the plane.

Holding the seat firmly in place is important no matter how you plan to cut away the wood. I usually use the bandsawn cutoffs between bench dogs to hold the seat in place on my workbench. You could also make a simple holder from a piece of plywood with some blocks screwed to it, adding some wedges to hold the seat tightly in place. Clamp or screw this to a sturdy worktable.

Where do you begin? To avoid cutting into the area around the leg joints, mark a border area around the back and sides of the seat to remain uncut. Then start removing wood in the area of the tail bones (see the photo above). The tail is one big hollow. This is where the seat is the deepest and where you'll need to do

The pile of shavings is growing, and it's starting to look a little more like a seat.

the most work. In general, you want to work on the deeper areas first, then spread out to the shallower places. Try to work symmetrically. There is no need to actually count strokes, but be aware that you're looking for balanced results, and this takes balanced effort. Once you're starting to achieve some depth (see the photo above), start cutting the separate hollows for the legs. Leave a ridge between the legs. It helps to mark a line from the front edge about 9 in. long, centered on the seat. Scoop out wood only to either side of the line.

The high point of the slope down into the seat hollow begins about 3½ in. back from the front of the seat. Forward of this point, the leg hollows get deeper. This is more comfortable for the backs of your legs.

Defining the ridge is a more delicate process than hacking away at the wood. The ridge line needs to be straight and clearly defined. It also needs to grow out of the tail hollow.

Sitting in a seat with a ridge that extends too far back is quite uncomfortable. Cut a flat on the top of the ridge toward the back so it slopes a little with the hollows for the legs. Work slowly and carefully from both sides to redefine it.

The best way to test your work is to sit down on the seat frequently, figure out where you still need to remove wood, and then remove it. (You'll probably want to sit down often anyway—there's a lot of wood to remove.) Keep going until you have something that is both comfortable and interesting to look at. Try for a depth of at least ¾ in. in the center of the tail hollow. Put a straightedge across the seat to help measure the depth as you go.

I start the smoothing process with a random-orbit sander (or even a sanding pad chucked in a drill) with coarse, 40-grit sandpaper (see the left photo on the facing page). Pay particular attention to high spots and tearout, but you still need to cover the whole seat evenly. This does a

Sand the seat with a random-orbit sander, starting with 40-grit sandpaper.

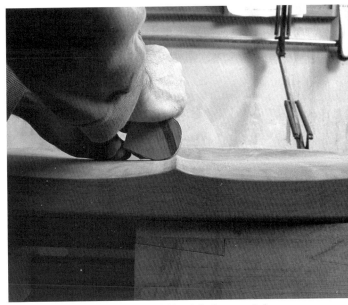

Hand-sanding with a curved block helps straighten and define the ridge.

surprisingly good job, but there is still a lot of hand work necessary. The ridge, in particular, must be worked carefully to keep the line crisp and straight. I like using curved sanding blocks (see the right photo above) and occasionally a curved scraper. Sand immediately adjacent to the ridge on both sides, working parallel to the ridge. As you even out the areas next to the ridge, the ridge itself will get straighter.

The very back of the seat hollow is also difficult to smooth out evenly. Work this with a curved sanding block, too, but work across the grain. Then go back to the random-orbit sander to take care of the cross-grain scratches.

Use your fingers as well as your eyes to check your work. Once the seat seems smooth, brush off the sawdust and grit, and go over it with a scraper to level out the remaining irregularities. Spring the scraper to whatever curve is necessary. This is not a typical sequence, but it works. The sanded surface looks very differ-

ent from the scraped one, and small hollows are easy to spot. After scraping, I sand with finer and finer grits, constantly checking by sight and touch. Look at the seat from a low angle, and move your fingers both slowly and quickly to test the seat more critically. Once the finish is applied, any uneven areas will become much more obvious.

Sand the remaining flat areas with a sanding block, carefully avoiding the areas around the leg joints. Then sand from the flat areas into the seat hollow, easing the transition consistently. When you're satisfied, move on to the edges and the bottom of the seat.

Now is the time to give the seat blank its final shape prior to assembly. Draw the curve of the back of the seat, using the lines drawn from the rear legs to locate the ends of the curve. Redraw the curves on the sides of the seat to fit the legs exactly, bandsaw the seat to shape, and sand the edges smooth. Attach the legs again to be sure everything lines up as it should, then round over all but the last 2 in. to either side of the rear legs and the curved front edge with a ¼-in. radius bit. Work on the final fit of the transition areas around the rear legs after assembly. Sand everything even and smooth.

Shaping the legs

The front legs are the easiest to shape. Plane, scrape, and sand all of the surfaces. Then round the edges with a ¼-in. roundover bit. This works even on the curved faces of the legs because the curves are gentle. The rounded-over edges work well in conjunction with the leg-to-seat joints. Unfortunately, this is not the case for all of the other joints on the chair.

After the surfaces on the rear legs are smoothed, you can round over portions of the legs, but there is an area that you should avoid. Stop a couple of inches short of the arm notches (both above and below and on the front and the back). Once the chair is together, you can gradually reduce the rounding of the edges as they approach the joints with the arms.

Shaping the arms

The basic planing, scraping, and sanding are easily done on the arms alone. Dry-assemble the chair to mark and rough out what needs to be done where the arms join the rear legs. But wait until after assembly to do the final work on these areas.

The very back of the arm should be marked and cut just proud of the back of the rear leg. At the front of the rear leg, mark the arm so you can start on the gradual twist that enables the arm to meet the leg precisely. Make sure that any other shaping doesn't affect the fit of the arm in the leg notch. Round over all but the last 2 in. (on all four edges) at the backs of the arms.

Shaping the back slat

The basic shape of the back slat has already been cut on the bandsaw; a little more shaping remains, along with general smoothing and rounding the edges. Hold the slat in place for smoothing supported by the cutoff between bench dogs. If you don't have a compass plane, the best approach is to sand the concave surface using a sanding block cut to the curve of the back. The outside surface can be planed with a smooth plane, then sanded. Check the shape of the slat against the legs to be sure there is an even setback and that the slat doesn't extend into the rounded part of the leg.

Since the back slat looked too rectilinear, I added a gentle curve to the top and bottom edges, about ⅜ in. up at the center. I cut this on the bandsaw, supporting the slat with a cutoff. The curve could just be planed and spokeshaved (or even sanded) as well. With the slat back in place, sit down in the chair once again to feel if any part of the slat needs work. Then finish sanding the slat smooth, and round the edges with the ¼-in. roundover bit.

ASSEMBLING THE CHAIR

Since all of the joints except those for the back slat have screws, this is a relatively peaceful glue-up. You may still need clamps to draw the interlocking joints tight if they need a little extra persuasion—this process could otherwise snap the screws—but the screws will hold things tight once everything is together.

It helps to assemble the chair up off the floor; support the seat securely and at a comfortable working height. Get everything you'll need for the assembly together. Then start with the front legs. Spread glue sparingly on both sides of the inner notch, then push or clamp the legs and seat together, and drive in the screws. The rear legs are next. Start with just one of the legs. Spread glue, push or gently tap the leg into place (with a soft-faced mallet), then screw. Apply glue in the slat mortises in both legs and sparingly on the slat tenons, and insert the appropriate tenon into the attached leg mortise. Then work on getting the other leg into place and screwed tight. Clamp across the slat both front and back for more even pressure. The arms are last. Spread glue in the mortise, lightly on the tenon of the front leg, and in the rear leg notch, but not on the back of the arm to avoid smearing glue on the leg. Place the arm onto the front leg tenon, and clamp from the bottom of the leg to seat the joint if necessary. Work the back of the arm into the notch, and screw.

Once everything is together, plug all of the holes with either matching or contrasting wood. If you're trying to match, cut plugs from the cutoffs that came from the specific area on the legs that you're plugging. For contrast, you can either use end-grain plugs, which will finish up darker, or cut the plugs from a different wood. A darker wood is the usual choice because lighter woods may stand out too much. Once the plugs are glued into place, cut and sand them flush.

THE FINISHING TOUCHES

Now it's time to deal with the work that has been postponed until after the final assembly. Start with sanding the back of the seat to fit the legs. I used a belt sander for the initial work here, then followed up with hand-sanding to eliminate the bumps I put in with the sander. Move on to "feathering" the rounded-over edges

Note how the rounded edges "feather" into some intersections. This is most visible where the seat joins the rear leg.

as they approach various joints: the back of the seat into the legs (see the photo above), the insides of the arms into the rear legs, and the rear legs into the arms. Finally, sand the backs of the arms flush with the backs of the legs.

Apply your choice of finish (see the appendix on p. 195 for my oil and wax finish), tack on glides, and pull up a chair.

10
ARMCHAIRS

aving made one chair, the next step is usually to make a set of chairs. And most often, a set of chairs includes two armchairs. Adding arms to any chair design is not too hard. But there are some structural considerations and some design issues to ponder. After discussing these, I'll offer a quick "how to" for adding arms to one of the chairs in the book.

ARMCHAIR STRUCTURE

Although there are countless varieties of arms and arm structures on chairs, there are only two standard types: arms that attach to extended front legs (such as on the captain's chair in Chapter 9) and those that attach to arm posts that extend

up from the side rails (such as on the chair in the photo on the facing page).

Extended front legs

I prefer extending the front legs because it adds significantly to the overall strength of the chair and makes a stronger arm as well. This is also a cleaner look, and so it is usually preferred on more modern chair designs.

There are a few minor changes to think about when building an armchair with extended legs. You can make some alterations in the rail-to-leg joinery. Since we don't have to worry about the mortises coming too close to the top of the leg, we can cut the mortises a little bit wider. This gives us joints with larger glue surfaces.

I like to cut and shape the front leg from wider stock to create a little more room between the arms (see the drawing on p. 186). This is both a visual and a practical issue. I prefer an inviting or open look to the arms, but there also must be enough room for a heavier or more heavily clothed person to fit between the arms. On wider chairs, a straight leg can be extended up with good results.

The mortise-and-tenon joint is the most common front-leg-to-arm joint (outside of the dowels used in industry). But mortise-and-tenon joinery is not the only option. If the leg flows into the arm, a bridle joint or even finger joints may be appropriate.

Jonathan Binzen

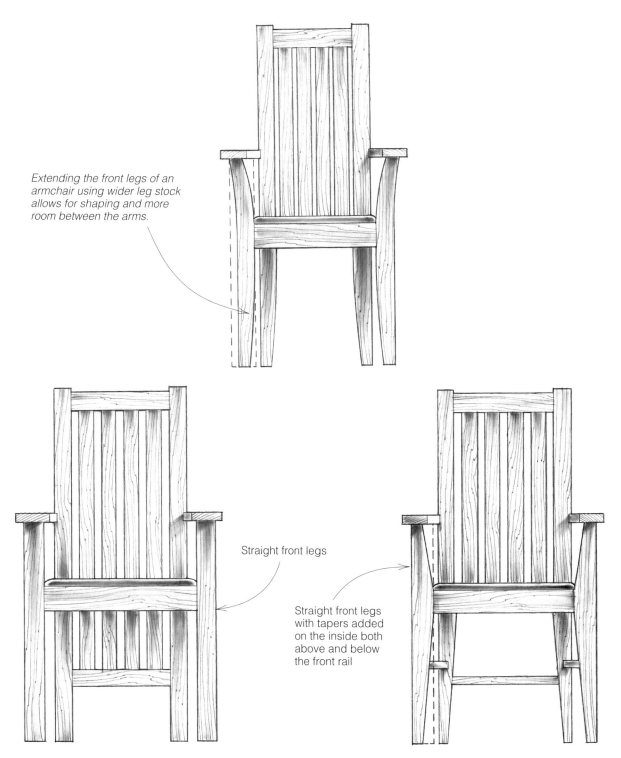

Extending the front legs of an armchair using wider leg stock allows for shaping and more room between the arms.

Straight front legs

Straight front legs with tapers added on the inside both above and below the front rail

Front legs can be cut from square leg stock on a wider chair.

POSSIBILITIES FOR ATTACHING THE ARM TO THE BACK LEG

Arm attached to side of leg

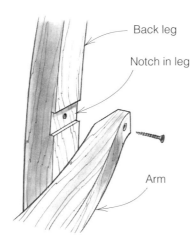

The arm could also be screwed from the inside of the leg.

Arm tenoned to front of leg

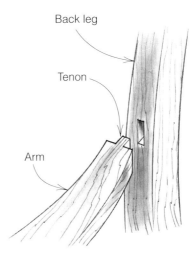

Arm attached to corner of leg

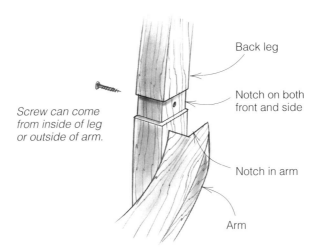

Screw can come from inside of leg or outside of arm.

You can attach the back of the arm to the rear leg in many different ways (see the drawing above). The easiest is to screw and glue the arm to the side of the rear leg. Screws by themselves are not an ideal joint in this situation, however. You can add considerably to the strength of the arm by doing something to absorb the shearing forces that will be exerted on this joint. Cutting a shallow notch in the leg for the arm is a big help (see p. 174).

You can also attach the arm to the front of the leg. I do this only on wider chairs, where the issue of enough room for the back between the arms doesn't exist (see the photo on p. 185). Use a mortise-and-tenon joint (oriented vertically) in this situation. You will usually have to angle the tenon to fit the back. This generally works well even if the back is slightly curved, although you may have to plane a small flat to get a perfect fit (or use a little filler afterward). This creates a very strong arm.

Joining the arm to the corner of the rear leg is also a possibility. Obviously the arm must be notched for this. If you can notch the leg as well, you'll add a lot of strength.

There are two additional issues that relate to the seat blank. The first may be completely obvious, but the seat blank must be notched in the front corners for the front legs. Leave about $\frac{3}{32}$ in. of space around the leg to allow for the upholstery fabric and batting. An upholsterer will have no trouble with the notch. The second issue can be a rather nasty surprise. It can be very difficult to get an upholstered seat into position

with arms in the way (especially with extended straight legs). I've never actually been unable to attach the seat, but I have had to work hard on numerous occasions. This is an advantage to a true slip seat—one recessed in a rabbet on the rails—because the seat blank will be slightly smaller.

Arm posts from the side rails
On many traditional chairs, the arms are attached to arm posts that are added to the side rails (see the drawing below). This method is more complicated than extending the front legs, and it also requires more work to ensure that it is strong enough. Typically, there is also a lot more shaping of both arm and arm post than with extended front legs. One advantage is that the arms can be shorter, allowing the chair to fit in closer to a table and lessening the chance of smashing fingers into an apron under the table.

POSSIBILITIES FOR ARM POSTS AND ARMS

Arm attached to arm post attached to side rail

More refined arm/arm post possibilities

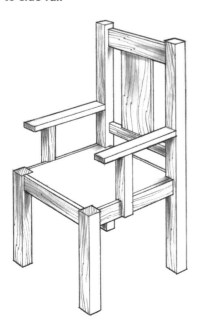

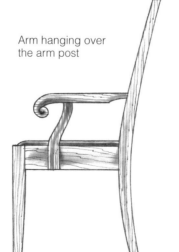

Arm hanging over the arm post

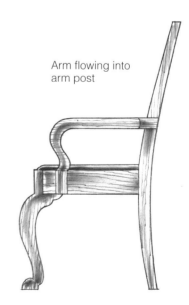

Arm flowing into arm post

In addition to the issues of attaching the arm to the rear leg discussed already, the arm post must be attached securely to the side rail. As with the rear-leg-to-arm joint, simply screwing the arm post to the rail is less than ideal. Adding a notch to either the post, the leg, or both is a big help. On better chairs, the arm post is often dovetailed into the rail, and then screwed (see the drawing below). If there isn't enough thickness to the rail for this, a reinforcing block can be added inside.

There is an additional issue to consider with arm posts. Because they attach to the side rails and the side rails are usually at an angle to the rear legs, the arm post will also be at an angle to the back legs. This is not really a problem. If the arm itself is cut from a slightly larger blank, this angle is easily accommodated in shaping and joining the arm.

The options for joining arm to arm post are the same as for joining arm to front leg.

ARMCHAIR DESIGN

I mentioned some of the basic design parameters for arms on chairs in Chapter 1, but I'll repeat and expand a little on that here. There are four main parameters: arm height, distance between the arms, arm length, and arm width. Of these, arm height and distance between the arms are the most important. I try to keep arm height between 7 in. and 8½ in. above the seat. An inch or two higher is also comfortable but tends to interfere with table aprons. The distance between arms has to be enough to allow someone to sit down comfortably. And at the back of the chair, there must be enough room to avoid pinching the back. This translates into a distance of 18 in. to 20 in. at the front of the

ATTACHING THE ARM POST TO THE SIDE RAIL SECURELY

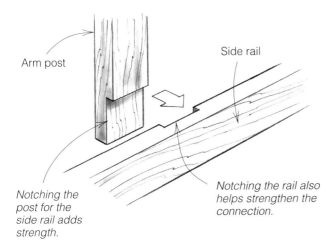

Arm post

Side rail

Notching the post for the side rail adds strength.

Notching the rail also helps strengthen the connection.

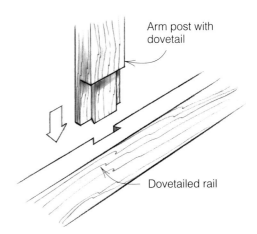

Arm post with dovetail

Dovetailed rail

This armchair version of the author's slat-back chair (see p. 104) has front legs cut from wider leg blanks. The arms here are just ¼-in. plywood patterns.

arm support is 12 in. Arm width tends to be variable, especially because arms often get wider toward the front of the chair. (This is friendlier to the hands.) I try to support the sitter's arms with a chair arm width of at least 1¾ in. to 2 in.

Keep in mind that in practice, chairmakers do not stick closely to these guidelines, preferring to place more weight on the appearance of the arms. It's not surprising that issues of comfort are often ignored when designing the arms—it's not easy to get them to look right. First of all, the arms must belong with the chair—they have to look like an integral part of the design. This means that the shapes should relate to the rest of the chair, if possible. Arms should also look open and inviting. Parallel arms or arms that curve inward can actually look pinched and closed (the same problem we saw with perspective on the right-angle chair with parallel sides). Walk around a chair to see what the arms look like from all angles. Some curves look strange from certain angles, and this is not something you want to discover after the chair is done.

MAKING AN ARMCHAIR

Now that I've created the impression that making an armchair is a difficult task, I'd like to counter that with a basic discussion of how to make a slat-back armchair. You could easily apply this to the right-angle chair or even the café chair if desired. I will limit my comments to the things that are different about making the armchair. I will also describe an easier version of the armchair. With a wider chair or one with a greater front-to-back taper, this version may be preferable anyway.

chair, or possibly an inch or two wider. At the back of the chair, 15 in. is a minimum. To increase the distance between arms on chairs that need a bit more room, I will either taper the inside of the front leg above the rail or shape the leg from thicker stock.

The issues of arm length and width are less critical. With extended front legs, the arm length is whatever it takes to get from back to front. With arm posts, there is a trade-off between supporting the whole arm and allowing the sitter to sit closer to a table. A good minimum length for

There is really only one thing that must be done differently right from the start in making this armchair—the front legs (see the photo on the facing page). To gain a little more room between the arms and to create a more open look to the armchair, cut and shape the legs from wider blanks (see the drawing at right). Rather than cutting the legs from 1½-in. squares, the armchair legs use 1½-in. by 2½-in. stock. Cut the legs 23¾ in. long, and mortise them as you would for the side chair. If you reference off the inside faces, the mortising is a little less confusing. The tenons on top of the legs are next. I like to angle these down toward the back 2 or 3 degrees because I like the way the space between the arm and the side rail looks this way. But the arms might actually be a little more comfortable left perpendicular to the front legs because they would be slightly higher in back.

You can experiment with the angle of the arm by cutting the tenons square and just tilting the arms up and down until you find a look that you like. Then make a wedge to give you this angle, and recut the tenons using the wedge.

Once the joints are cut, lay out and cut the front legs to shape. As with shaping the back legs, be careful to avoid tapering or rounding the rail flats. Leave enough room to clean up any uneven lines cut on the bandsaw. You can usually clean up the longer tapers on the jointer, but you'll need to plane, scrape, and/or sand the curved outsides of the legs and the short tapers above the rails.

When everything else on the chair is ready, dry-assemble the basic frame, and clamp it tight. (You don't need to put the slats in to proceed with this.) You need to determine three

PATTERNS FOR FRONT LEGS AND ARMS

Scale: 1 square = 1 in.

Bottom view of arm

Front view of front leg

Side view of front leg

Leave extra wood here so you can fit the curve exactly to the rear leg.

⅜-in. x 1-in. tenon

1¼ in.

1 in.

Front of leg

Outside of leg

19 in.

Approximate location of mortise (mortise can be longer if desired)

Arm

23¾ in.

4 in.

1-in.-thick arm blank

Approximate location of mortise

Front leg blank

1 in.

1 in.

See the drawing on p. 106 for the basic slat-back chair parts.

Mark the location of the mortise on the underside of the arm blank.

things: the size of the arm blanks, the location of the mortises on the blanks, and where the arms connect with the rear legs. (You need to do this only if you're going to notch the rear legs for the arms.) Since the front and rear legs are parallel, we don't have to make up the same sort of template we used for the captain's chair in Chapter 9. Instead, clamp an arm blank—roughly 4 in. by 20 in. by 1 in. thick—to the outside of one of the rear legs and slightly proud of the back of the leg. Then mark the location of the mortise underneath (see the photo at left).

You will need to mortise an arm blank to accurately figure out where the arm will connect with the rear leg. Don't cut the mortise exactly where you marked it. Shift it $1/32$ in. toward the outside of the blank. This will compensate for the $1/32$-in.-deep notch you will cut on the rear leg. Fit the tenon to the mortise, if neces-

sary, then clamp the arm blank to the front leg. At the rear leg, clamp the arm blank to the leg, and scribe lines both top and bottom across the side of the leg (see the bottom photo on the facing page). Then disassemble the chair, and rout and chisel the notch $1/16$ in. deep (see p. 177 for details on how to do this accurately).

Mark out, cut, and smooth the arms, leaving a little extra wood where the pilot holes for the screws will be drilled. Then proceed with the assembly of the rest of the chair. On this chair, the arms go on after everything else is together. This means that the arms must be screwed and plugged to the legs from the outside. I prefer this anyway because there is more wood for the screw to hold in the leg. But some situations call for screwing from the inside of the legs into the arms. In a case like that, you might have to rethink the assembly

EXPERIMENTING WITH ARM SHAPES

If you want to experiment with arm shapes, you should make up a bunch of $1/4$-in. plywood patterns before you start cutting arm blanks. Clamp a small block to the rear leg so you have a way to clamp the patterns there (see the photo at right). The arms can rest on top of the tenon in front—using tape if necessary—since that will be the actual arm height. Make up the patterns in pairs so you can get a sense of what the chair will look like with both arms in place.

Try out different shapes for the arms using $1/4$-in. plywood patterns. This is a shape I ultimately rejected for this chair.

sequence completely, or angle the screw so that there is room to drive the screws in and plug the holes.

Counterbore holes, spread glue in the arm mortises and lightly on the tenons and in the rear leg notches, and install the arms. Clamp the front of the arms down, and screw the back of the arms to the rear legs. Then plug the screw holes, and sand the back of the arms to their finished shape.

For the simpler version of the armchair, the arms are not offset to the outside as much (see the photo at right). Cut the front legs from square stock, and mortise as above. Offset the tenon to the outside of the leg. Then taper the leg both above and below the rails. On the slat-back chair, I think this version is a little less effective. The arms just don't have quite enough room to curve outward as gracefully. But I have done other, wider chairs this way, and I think it works well for them (see the photo on p. 185 and the drawing on p. 186).

Having completed an armchair, we come to the close of our chair études. I hope that this is just the beginning of your exploration and enjoyment of chairmaking.

This version of the slat-back armchair has square front legs with a simple taper.

Mark the rear legs with a sharp knife to locate the shallow arm notches. This knife has a bevel on one side only so it cuts exactly in line with the arm.

AFTERWORD

THOUGHTS ON DEVELOPING NEW CHAIR DESIGNS

If few people attempt to make chairs, even fewer attempt to design them. But the process of design, although it involves a fair bit of work, is one of the most rewarding and exciting processes.

How does a new design begin? Most often with a concept, an idea for modification, or a question (what if I tried that with...?); sometimes with a vague image; and only rarely with real inspiration. But whatever the beginning, what follows is experimentation. I usually start with sketches, but I am admittedly not very good at transferring my ideas onto paper. Even if you can draw well, the next step is some sort of mock-up. The trick with the early stages of experimenting with a design is to work efficiently (that is, quickly and cheaply). You want to be able to look at your idea and consider it critically, even if you have to squint a little to hide the obvious defects. And you want to be able to do this with minimal investment. This requires real creativity—how resourceful can you be when the challenge is to test out your idea? If one shape doesn't work, try taping some paper or cardboard over what you have to try out a different shape. If you need to change the height, prop something underneath. What do you have handy that can support a plywood chair seat at the right height?

The first mock-up may not even be sittable. Many designers like working with a scale model to play around with an idea. This lets them hold it in their hands and consider it from every angle. I tend to have a lot of scrap around, so I work with that. But other materials serve the purpose as well—for example, 2-in.-thick Styrofoam is available at lumberyards and cuts and shapes incredibly quickly.

Once you can see your idea, start to ask questions. Does the chair look good (or can it be made to look good)? Does it look like the structure will hold together? If not, what methods might be used to make it work? Is the chair going to be comfortable? Another mock-up may be necessary to test out questions you can't answer yet. You may require yet another completely different mock-up to work out construction details. This was the case for me with the café chair—with curves joining curves, I had to work out methods that would accommodate my ideas for comfort and appearance. Among the most important elements of design at this stage are patience and perseverance.

Once you've settled on a basic design, there are still other questions to ask. Should the construction methods express some of the visual concept, or should the structure remain hidden and subservient to the design? Is there anything that should be added or taken away from the design? This is an important question, and the answers tell you if you are getting somewhere with the design. If nothing can be added without looking superfluous, and nothing can be taken away without diminishing the design in some way, you have done your work well.

In many respects, successful design means being able to objectively criticize your own ideas. I like to look over my designs slowly and carefully, searching for weaknesses. I walk around the chair; I consider it from high up and down low, from near and far. Things that don't make sense, that are not balanced and well proportioned, that I don't feel comfortable with, and that really aren't what I had in mind, I try to change. Don't worry—you can't fix everything, and you probably can't fix more than one or two problems at a time. Most good designs go through many changes and are refined over different versions. This may seem discouraging at first. But in design, as in almost everything else, the more you try, the more you learn.

The more you practice your critical skills—both in your own work and in that of others—the more you will see in your own work and in the designs around you. Going through the design process yourself will supply you with even more critical and creative tools.

APPENDIX

AN OIL AND WAX FINISH

After going through all of the fun and trouble of making your chair, you'll want to finish it well. There are countless options, and I will ignore all but two of them: an oil and wax finish and a lacquer finish.

If you are experienced with spraying lacquer, there is no need for me—a relatively inexperienced amateur when it comes to spray finishes—to tell you what to do. If you opt for lacquer and have little experience with it, find someone to finish for you, or find a good book on the topic to get you started. Spraying lacquer safely requires a good spray booth and a respirator, along with all of the necessary spray equipment. The new water-based lacquers can be sprayed much more safely, but I've found them less forgiving than nitrocellulose lacquer and a little less rich-looking as well.

An oil and wax finish is easily applied at home with no special equipment. The finish is less resistant to water and staining than lacquer, but it is much easier to maintain. You see and feel the wood surface, not a film over it. An oil and wax finish is usually not as formal-looking as lacquer, but it is still beautiful and rich. I use a thinned oil-and-varnish blend commonly known as Danish oil.

To start, examine your chairs closely for imperfections: dents, glue spots, and so forth. Try to spot and correct any problems *before* you start the finishing process. You will be able to work on problems later but not without some extra effort. For safety, wear gloves when finishing, and work in a well-ventilated area, wearing a respirator with an organic compounds filter.

Apply the first coat of oil with a small rag. Get the wood evenly wet— be generous with the oil. Most of this will probably be absorbed into the wood quite rapidly. Rewet the entire surface with more oil. Let the oil soak in for about 15 minutes, then wipe it off thoroughly with a clean rag. Pay particular attention to where pieces join because it is harder to wipe there. Let the chair sit overnight.

Dispose of your oily rags safely! Oily rags spontaneously combust. Place rags in water, and then in an airtight container, such as an empty can. Put the can away from other combustibles. The one night I left some oily rags bunched up in a bucket, I came in the next morning to a shop full of smoke and a smoldering heap of rags. I was lucky that was all that happened.

The second coat of oil is wet sanded. Start by applying a good soaking coat with a fresh rag, as with the first coat. Then wet sand with 220-grit or 320-grit wet-or-dry sandpaper, sanding only with the grain. Put a little oil on the sandpaper as well. Wipe off after only a few minutes, sooner than with the first coat. Let sit overnight.

The third coat is sanded just like the second coat but with a finer-grit paper (320 or 400). After you've wiped the piece off, let it sit for a half hour or so, and then wipe it down again with a clean rag. Depending on the wood, you may have to wipe the piece a few more times if the oil comes back to the surface. Again, pay particular attention to the joints and other hard-to-wipe places. Any oil left on the surface will turn gummy and will be harder to deal with once dry. Let sit overnight.

Wax the piece with a good furniture-quality paste wax. Apply just a little bit of wax at a time with a pad of extra fine, 0000 steel wool, rubbing in well with the grain. Be fairly stingy with the wax. You do want some on the piece, but not much. And what you put on should be evenly applied. Buff with a soft cloth. You may need to go back with a clean pad of steel wool or a fine plastic abrasive pad, and rub the finish again to even it out. The result should be very smooth and lustrous.

MAINTAINING THE FINISH

To clean or dust the wood, I use a few drops of lemon oil on a rag. (The same oily rag disposal precautions apply here, too.) The lemon oil really doesn't do much more than clean, however. To restore the finish if it is damaged or just looking dry, oil once again with the Danish oil, wiping dry carefully. Wax if you find it's necessary to restore the luster and the feel of the freshly finished piece.

INDEX

PUBLISHER   James P. Chiavelli

ACQUISITIONS EDITOR   Rick Peters

PUBLISHING COORDINATOR   Joanne Renna

EDITOR   Nancy Nickum Bailey

LAYOUT ARTIST   Lynne Phillips

ILLUSTRATOR   David Dann

PHOTOGRAPHER   Tanya Tucka (except where noted)

INDEXER   Harriet Hodges

TYPEFACE   Garamond

PAPER   70 lb. Patina

PRINTER   Quebecor Printing/Hawkins, New Canton, Tennessee